CAREERS FOR

COLOR CONNOISSEURS

& Other Visual Types

Careers for You Series

CAREERS FOR

COLOR CONNOISSEURS

& Other Visual Types

JAN GOLDBERG

SECOND EDITION

McGraw-Hill

New York Chicago San Francisco Lisbon London Madrid Mexico City
Milan New Delhi San Juan Seoul Singapore Sydney Toronto

The *McGraw·Hill* Companies

Library of Congress Cataloging-in-Publication Data

Goldberg, Jan
      Careers for color connoisseurs & other visual types / Jan Goldberg — 2nd ed.
        p.   cm. — (McGraw-Hill careers for you series)
        ISBN 0-07-143855-6 (alk. paper)
        1. Art—Vocational guidance.   2. Design—Vocational guidance.   I. Title:
      Careers for color connoisseurs and other visual types.   II. Title.   III. Series.

      N8350.G65   2005
      702'.3—dc22   2004019678

1 2 3 4 5 6 7 8 9 0   DOC/DOC   0 9 8 7 6 5

ISBN 0-07-143855-6

McGraw-Hill books are available at special quantity discounts to use as premiums and sales promotions, or for use in corporate training programs. For more information, please write to the Director of Special Sales, Professional Publishing, McGraw-Hill, Two Penn Plaza, New York, NY 10121-2298. Or contact your local bookstore.

This book is printed on acid-free paper.

*This book is dedicated to the memory
of my beloved parents,
Sam and Sylvia Lefkovitz,
and to a dear aunt, Estelle Lefko.*

Contents

	Acknowledgments	ix
CHAPTER ONE	**Choosing Your Color Palette**	1
CHAPTER TWO	**Designers**	13
CHAPTER THREE	**Studio Artists**	33
CHAPTER FOUR	**Commercial Artists**	51
CHAPTER FIVE	**Art Museum Professionals**	69
CHAPTER SIX	**Art Gallery Professionals**	91
CHAPTER SEVEN	**Art Educators**	97
CHAPTER EIGHT	**Other Colorful Careers**	111
APPENDIX	**Trade, Industrial, and Vocational Schools**	119

Acknowledgments

The author gratefully acknowledges the following individuals for their contributions to this project:

- The numerous professionals who graciously agreed to be profiled in this book
- My dear husband, Larry, for his inspiration and vision
- My children, Deborah, Bruce, and Sherri, for their encouragement and love
- Family and close friends—Adrienne, Marty, Mindi, Cary, Michele, Paul, Michele, Alison, Steve, Marci, Steven, Brian, Jesse, Bertha, Uncle Bernard, and Aunt Helen—for their faith and support
- Diana Catlin, for her insights and input

The editors wish to thank Brad Crawford for revising this second edition.

CHAPTER ONE

Choosing Your Color Palette

Colors speak all languages.
—Joseph Addison

You're a color connoisseur, an artiste, a lover of hues and tints, shades and tones. You take your environment seriously, and your moods are affected by the colors around you. You choose your clothes and your home decorations with thoughtful care to the harmony—or planned discord—that different colors create. You're happiest when your surroundings reflect your preferences, when you're able to make an individual statement.

As with all visual types, you dream in vivid Technicolor, and some of those dreams involve finding a career in which you can combine your love of color and a way to earn a living.

Color connoisseurs, true artists at heart, find ways to express themselves through many media and in a variety of settings. If you're reading this book, chances are you're already considering a career in this wide-open category.

Exploring the Possibilities

Let's look at the many job titles open to you and the settings in which these professionals find work. Many are explored in detail in the following chapters.

Art Educator, Art Teacher, Art Instructor

Those who can, do; those who can, also teach. Art educators instruct budding artists in the time-tested techniques and methods for creating art in a variety of media—from ceramics to computer graphics. Job settings include:

- Public and private schools
- Colleges and universities
- Adult education centers
- Private art studios
- Community centers
- Camps
- Parks and recreation departments
- Museums

Art Historian

Art historians delve deeply into the art of past and more recent cultures, then pass that knowledge on through their writings and teachings. Job settings include:

- Colleges and universities
- Museums

Art Conservator, Art Restorer

To some color connoisseurs, nothing is more important than rescuing a work of art from damage or decay. Art conservators, once known as art restorers, are trained in the painstaking methods used to repair artwork. Job settings include:

- Museums
- Art galleries
- Self-employment

Art Gallery Owner/Director, Art Curator

Art gallery staff must be articulate and knowledgeable about art history and current popular artists. One of the main responsibilities of a gallery owner or director is choosing which artists to feature and promote. Sales ability is also an asset.

A curator has many responsibilities, including choosing which art to display, how best to display it, and how to care for it. Curators in art museums are responsible for preserving the collection and implementing public access to view it. Job settings for curators and art gallery professionals include:

- Museums
- Art galleries
- Auction houses

Art Appraiser

Art appraisers are often art curators by training and experience. They draw on this experience to place a value on artwork that is on display in museums, privately owned, or up for sale at auction. They often study past sales to help with their evaluation. Job settings include:

- Museums
- Art galleries
- Auction houses

Exhibit Designer

Exhibit designers work closely with the curatorial staff and often with the education department to turn ideas into permanent or temporary exhibits. They use drawings, scale models, special lighting, and other techniques. Exhibit designers usually have formal training in graphic or industrial design, commercial art or communications arts, architecture, interior design, or studio arts. Job settings include:

- Museums
- Art galleries
- Large corporations

Registrar, Collections Manager

Registrars track all the works of art in a museum's collection, including works on display, in storage, in traveling exhibits, and on loan to other institutions. They also package artwork and arrange for shipping and insurance.

Collections managers are responsible for the objects within museum divisions or departments. They catalog each item and work with the registrar's office and the curatorial staff to maintain and exhibit the work. Job settings include:

- Museums
- Art galleries
- Private collections

Art Critic

Art critics help to shape public tastes with their opinions. They can help make or break an artist's career. Art critics must be knowledgeable of art history and current trends, and they must also be thick-skinned. An art critic isn't always popular. Job settings include:

- Newspapers
- Magazines
- Websites
- Self-employment

Visual Artist

Visual artists, which include studio (or fine) artists and graphic artists and illustrators, use an almost limitless variety of methods and materials to communicate ideas, thoughts, and feelings.

Studio artists usually specialize in one or two forms of art, which can include painting, photography, pottery, printmaking, sculpting, and stained glass. Graphic artists use a variety of print, electronic, and film media to create art that specifically meets a client's needs. Illustrators paint or draw pictures for books, magazines, and other publications; films; and paper products. Many do a variety of illustrations, while others specialize in a particular style. Job settings include:

- Art studios
- Advertising agencies
- Publishing houses
- Design firms
- Manufacturers
- Museums
- Retail stores
- Movie production companies
- Major corporations
- Self-employment

Fashion Designer

Fashion designers design clothing and accessories. Some "high-fashion" designers make fashion news by establishing new lines— the colors, styles, and kinds of materials that will be worn each season. Other fashion designers cater to specialty stores or high-fashion department stores. Most designers, though, work for manufacturers, creating mass-market fashions. Job settings for fashion designers include:

- Clothing manufacturers
- Design firms
- Self-employment

Color Consultant

Color plays an elemental role in the way we perceive the world around us. It affects our moods, motivation, and even appetites. It's no surprise, then, that color consultants figure prominently in many design occupations, from interior design to industrial design and packaging design. Color consultants use their knowledge about color compatibility, people's reactions to certain colors, and the suitability of different colors for specific purposes to maximize appeal. Job settings might include:

- Advertising agencies
- Architectural firms
- Design firms
- Retailers
- Self-employment

Other types of color consultants work in the beauty industry, helping individuals choose the best color combinations for their clothing and makeup. Job settings include:

- Department stores
- Beauty parlors/spas
- Hair salons

Cosmetologist, Makeup Artist, Esthetician

Cosmetologists, often called hair stylists, primarily shampoo, cut, and style hair. They also work with hair coloring. Most cosmetologists are also trained to give manicures and scalp and facial treatments, provide makeup analysis, and clean and style wigs and hairpieces. Makeup artists apply cosmetics. Estheticians work exclusively with skin care. Job settings include:

- Hair salons
- Beauty salons
- Movie and television companies
- Modeling agencies
- Department stores
- Self-employment

Wedding Consultant

Wedding consultants work with the bride and her family on particular aspects of planning the big event. Some consultants handle the entire affair, from choosing and ordering the flowers to arranging for catering and selecting the menu. Training ranges from go-at-your-own-pace correspondence courses to degree programs in events management. Job settings include:

- Hotels
- Bridal shops
- Self-employment

Interior Decorator, Interior Designer

Some color connoisseurs are in their element when they can discuss the dreams of others and bring them to fruition. Whether creating original tableaus or re-creating a glossy color magazine photo, designing and decorating the interior of homes requires talent as well as formal training. Job settings include:

- Architectural firms
- Furniture stores
- Private design firms
- Self-employment

Floral Designer, Florist

Nature created the most beautiful colors of all, and floral designers learn how to arrange them in pleasing displays. They custom-make arrangements to the specific needs of the client or design their own creations for sale or competition. Job settings for floral designers and florists include:

- Florist shops
- Grocery stores
- Nurseries
- Hospital gift shops
- Self-employment

Landscape Architect, Landscape Designer

Landscape architects and designers bring their love of color outdoors, choosing just the right combination of plants and flowers that thrive in a variety of climates and conditions. Landscape architects and landscape designers pursue different levels of educational training, but both combine artistic and scientific principles in designing both natural and planned environments. Job settings for landscape architects and landscape designers include:

- Landscape firms
- General contracting companies
- Architects
- Real estate development firms
- Municipalities and other government entities
- Nurseries
- Self-employment

Choosing the Right Field

Now that you've read descriptions of many jobs open to color connoisseurs, perhaps you're curious about which area would best suit your personality, skills, and lifestyle. Each field carries with it different levels of responsibility and commitment. To identify occupations that match your expectations, you need to know what each job entails.

Ask yourself the following questions and note your answers. Then, as you read the following chapters, compare your requirements to the information provided by the professionals interviewed. Their comments will help you pinpoint the fields that would interest you and eliminate those that would clearly be the wrong choice.

- How much time are you willing to commit to training? Some skills come naturally; others require time and patience to master. Some employers will accept a candidate on the basis of a portfolio; others require evidence of formal training.
- Do you want to work on your own in a home studio, or would you prefer to be in a busy, more stimulating environment with other color connoisseurs and related experts near you?
- Can you handle a certain amount of stress on the job? Are you comfortable with deadlines and competition? Or do you prefer a quiet, work-at-your-own-pace environment?
- Do you need the security of a regular paycheck, or can you handle the uncertainty that comes with self-employment? How much money do you expect to earn starting out? How much after you have a few years' experience under your belt? Salaries and earnings vary greatly in each chosen profession.

Knowing what your expectations are and then comparing them to the realities of the work will help you make informed choices.

Training and Qualifications

Because the careers in which color connoisseurs can exercise their talents vary so greatly, it is understandable that the requirements and qualifications for employment are also varied. More and more professional jobs require at least a bachelor's degree. Highlighted in the chapters ahead, however, are some professions, such as studio art and floral design, that require applicants to have specialized skills rather than diplomas.

Choosing a Course of Study

If you decide to pursue formal training, you will soon discover that there are almost as many different names and focuses for art and art-related educational programs as there are job possibilities. Some of the common program names are Applied Arts, Fine Arts, Computer Arts, Computer-Aided Design, Studio Art, Art Education, Art History, Museum Studies, Commercial Art, Graphic Arts, Industrial Arts, Design, Communication Arts, and Visual Arts.

Many university programs allow for a great deal of latitude in designing majors and courses of study. It is now common practice to pursue interdisciplinary degrees. With a little bit of guidance and creativity, you should be able to pursue a program tailor-made to your future career choice.

The institutes, colleges, and universities that offer art as a major often categorize art and design departments in a variety of ways. In some institutions you will find the art department within the college of liberal arts or the humanities department. Others have separate art schools. Still others combine art programs with the school of architecture or with advertising, public relations, or other related disciplines.

The program or department name will not always be an accurate clue to its focus. For example, a potential art teacher would waste precious time enrolling in an art studies program that emphasized commercial art or design, because most teaching positions won't require those skills, and in any case schools usually look for teachers with degrees in art education.

If you are interested in teaching, you must make additional decisions. Should you pursue a B.F.A. in your chosen subject area, then work toward a teaching credential? Or should you study art education with a concentration in one of the subject areas? There is no one correct answer. You must arrive at your own answers based on your research into specific programs and your personal, long-term goals. Other considerations include the availability of programs within your area and whether you have the ability or funds to relocate if necessary.

One of the best ways to start is to narrow your choices through Web research. Then contact the various institutions you discover, send for catalogs, visit campuses, and talk to other students and faculty members. An informed decision about your training program will enhance your career opportunities.

Salaries

Just as the required qualifications for jobs differ, so do salaries. How much you'll earn will depend on your work setting, your employer, and your level of education and training, as well as the geographic area in which you live. Throughout the following chapters, you will learn more about typical salaries for professionals in each featured career.

For More Information

At the end of each chapter, you will find contact information for professional associations for many of the job titles discussed in this book. Most offer booklets and pamphlets with career information; others publish newsletters that list job openings. Much of the material is free, but some might have a nominal charge. A Web search, phone call, or e-mail will usually yield that information.

CHAPTER TWO

Designers

Art is not an end in itself, but a means of addressing humanity.
—M. P. Moussoughsky

Our world would be decidedly different without individuals who choose to design, for it is designers who make products, materials, and media visually pleasing while creating and organizing them so they serve the purpose for which they were intended. Pleasant surroundings, elegant clothes, and beautiful floral arrangements can boost our spirits, and eye-catching products and packaging are more likely to attract buyers.

A Look at Design

The first step in developing a new design or altering an existing one is to determine the needs of the client. The designer then considers various factors, including the size, shape, weight, and color of the product; the materials used in the product; and the product's functions. The ease of use, safety, and cost of the design are additional factors. Designers offer suggestions to their clients; some ideas are practical, while others are directed more to the aesthetics of the product. Designers then prepare illustrations of several design concepts. Clients could include an art or design director, a product development team, or the producer of a play, film, or television production.

The designer then makes a model (a prototype) or detailed plans drawn to scale. Designers in some specialties increasingly use computer-aided design (CAD) tools to create and better visualize a final product. Computers greatly reduce the cost and time necessary to create a model or prototype, which gives a real idea of what the product will look like. Industrial designers use computer-aided industrial design (CAID) to create designs and to communicate them to automated production tools.

Designers might supervise assistants who carry out their designs. Those who own businesses might also devote considerable time to developing new business contacts and to administrative tasks, such as reviewing catalogs and ordering samples.

Design Specialties

Many designers specialize in a particular area of design, such as automobiles, clothing, furniture, appliances, equipment, interiors, exhibits, movie and theater sets, packaging, or floral arrangements. Others work in more than one design field.

Industrial Designer

Industrial designers develop and design a multitude of manufactured products, including cars; home appliances; children's toys; computer equipment; and medical, office, and recreational equipment. They combine artistic talent with research on product use, marketing, materials, and production methods to create the most functional and appealing design and to make the product competitive in the marketplace.

Furniture Designer

Furniture designers design furniture for manufacture, based upon their knowledge of design trends, competitors' products, production costs, capability of production facilities, and the characteristics of a company's market. They might prepare detailed drawings of fixtures, forms, or tools required in the use of furniture production or be called upon to design custom pieces or styles according to a specific period or country. Furniture designers must be attuned to the fashion industry, as well, and aware of how current trends and styles affect the furniture market.

Interior Designer

Interior designers plan the space and furnish the interiors of private homes, public buildings, and commercial establishments. They might design offices, restaurants, hospitals, hotels, and theaters. They also might plan additions and renovations. Keeping a client's tastes, needs, and budget in mind, they develop designs and prepare working drawings and specifications for interior construction, furnishings, lighting, and furniture finishes. Increasingly, designers use computers to plan layouts that can be changed easily to include ideas received from the client.

Interior designers also design lighting and architectural details such as crown molding. They coordinate colors and select furniture, floor coverings, and curtains. Interior designers must design space in accordance with federal, state, and local laws and building codes. They also must ensure that designed public spaces meet accessibility standards for the disabled and elderly.

Set Designer

Set designers design movie, television, and theater sets. They study scripts, confer with directors, and conduct research to determine appropriate architectural styles.

Fashion Designer

Fashion designers design clothing and accessories. Some high-fashion designers are self-employed and design for individual clients. They make fashion news by establishing the "in" colors and kinds of materials that will be popular each season. Other high-fashion designers cater to specialty stores in high-fashion department stores. They design original garments as well as follow the established trends. Most fashion designers, however, work for apparel manufacturers, adapting men's, women's, and children's fashion for the mass market.

Textile Designer

Textile designers use their knowledge of materials and fashion trends to design fabric for garments, upholstery, rugs, and other products. Computers are widely used in pattern design.

Floral Designer

Floral designers cut live, dried, and artificial flowers and foliage and create arrangements that express customer sentiments. Their work might take the form of bouquets, sprays, wreaths, dish gardens, or terraria. They usually work from a written order indicating the occasion; the customer's preference for color and type of flower or plant; the price; and the date, time, and place of delivery. The variety of duties performed by a floral designer depends on the size of the shop and number of designers employed. In a small operation, the floral designer might own the shop and do almost everything, from growing flowers to keeping books.

Costume Designer

Costume designers design and create costumes for television and theatrical productions. They begin by reading the script before they meet with directors, lighting designers, and other professional staff. After these meetings, costume designers determine the number of costumes that each actor will need. They make a multitude of sketches and drawings to sharpen their ideas, and then they begin to choose fabrics and colors as the designs take shape. Costume designers are responsible for the wardrobes for the entire cast, including the lead actors, supporting actors, and extras.

Working Conditions

Working conditions and places of employment vary. Designers employed by manufacturing establishments or design firms generally work regular hours in well-lighted and comfortable settings. Self-employed designers tend to work longer hours—especially at first, when they are trying to establish themselves and cannot afford to hire assistants or clerical help.

Designers frequently adjust their workdays to suit their clients, meeting with them in the evenings or on weekends when necessary. They might transact business in their own offices or travel to clients' homes, offices, showrooms, or manufacturing facilities.

Industrial designers usually work regular hours but occasionally work overtime to meet deadlines. In contrast, set designers, especially those in television broadcasting, often work long and irregular hours. The pace of television production is very fast, and set designers are often under pressure to make rapid changes in the sets. Fashion designers who work in the apparel industry usually have regular hours. During production deadlines or before fashion shows, however, they might be required to travel to production sites overseas and across the United States. Interior designers generally work under deadlines and often work overtime to finish a job. Floral designers usually work regular hours in a pleasant environment, except for overtime during holidays.

All designers face frustrations—when they cannot be as creative as they wish or their designs are rejected. Independent consultants, who are paid by the assignment, are under pressure to please clients and to find new ones in order to maintain their income.

Job Settings

Nearly one-third of designers are self-employed, almost five times the rate for all professional and related occupations. Salaried designers work in a number of different industries, depending on their design specialty. Most industrial designers, for example, work for consulting firms or for large corporations.

Interior designers usually work for design or architectural firms, department stores and home furnishing stores, or hotel and restaurant chains. Many do freelance work—full-time, part-time, or in addition to a salaried job in another occupation.

Set designers work for theater companies and film and television production companies. Fashion designers generally work for textile, apparel, and pattern manufacturers, or for fashion salons, high-fashion department stores, and specialty shops. Some work in the entertainment industry designing costumes for theater, dance, television, or movies. Most floral designers work for retail flower shops, but a growing number work in the floral departments of grocery stores.

Training and Qualifications

Creativity is crucial in all design occupations. People in this field must have a strong sense of color, an eye for detail, a sense of balance and proportion, and sensitivity to beauty. Sketching ability is especially important for fashion designers. A good portfolio—a collection of examples of a person's best work—is often the deciding factor in getting a job. However, formal preparation in design is important in all fields, with the exception of floral design.

Educational requirements for entry-level positions vary. Some design occupations, notably industrial design, require a bachelor's degree. Interior designers also generally need a college education because few clients—especially commercial clients—are willing to entrust responsibility for designing living and working space to a designer with no formal credentials. Interior designers must also be knowledgeable about federal, state, and local codes and toxicity and flammability standards for furniture and furnishings.

Interior design is the only design field that is subject to government regulation. According to the American Society for Interior Designers, twenty-two states and the District of Columbia require interior designers to be licensed. To qualify, those designers must pass an examination administered by the National Council for Interior Design, which has a prerequisite of at least six years of combined education and experience in interior design (with at least two in postsecondary education). Because licensing is not mandatory in all states, membership in a professional association is universally recognized as a mark of achievement for interior designers.

In fashion design, some formal career preparation, such as a two- or four-year degree, is usually needed to enter the field. Employers seek individuals who are knowledgeable in the areas of textiles, fabrics, and ornamentation, as well as trends in the fashion world. Similarly, furniture designers must keep abreast of trends in fashion and style, in addition to methods and tools used in furniture production. A number of universities and schools of design offer degrees in furniture design.

In contrast to the other design occupations, the field of floral design is open to those with only a high school diploma. Most floral designers learn their skills on the job. When they hire trainees, employers generally look for high school graduates who have a flair for color and a desire to learn. However, completion of formal training is an asset for floral designers, particularly for advancement to the level of chief floral designer. Vocational and technical schools offer programs in floral design that last less than a year; two- and four-year programs in floriculture, horticulture, floral design, or ornamental horticulture are offered by community and junior colleges and four-year colleges and universities.

Formal training for some design professions is also available in two- and three-year professional schools that award certificates or associate degrees in design.

Graduates of two-year programs generally qualify as assistants to designers. The bachelor of arts degree is granted at four-year colleges and universities. The curriculum in these schools includes art and art history, principles of design, designing and sketching, and specialized studies for each of the individual design disciplines, such as garment construction, textiles, mechanical and architectural drawing, computerized design, sculpture, architecture, and basic engineering. A liberal arts education, with courses in merchandising, business administration, marketing, and psychology, along with training in art, is also a good background for most design fields. Individuals with training or experience in architecture also qualify for some design occupations, particularly interior design.

Computer-aided design (CAD) courses are very useful. CAD is used in various areas of design, and many employers expect new designers to be familiar with the use of the computer as a design tool. For example, industrial designers extensively use computers in the aerospace, automotive, and electronics industries. Interior designers use computers to create numerous versions of space designs. Images can be inserted, edited, or replaced, making it possible for a client to see and choose among several designs. In furniture design, a chair's basic shape and structure may be duplicated and updated by applying new upholstery styles and fabrics on the computer.

The National Association of Schools of Art and Design accredits more than two hundred postsecondary institutions with programs in art and design. Most of these schools award a degree in art. Some award degrees in industrial, interior, textile, graphic, or fashion design. Many schools do not allow formal entry into a bachelor's degree program until a student has successfully finished a year of basic art and design courses. Applicants may be required to submit sketches and other examples of their artistic ability.

The Foundation for Interior Design Education Research is the accrediting agency for interior design programs and schools. Currently, there are more than 120 accredited programs in schools of art, architecture, and home economics in the United States and Canada. Regardless of their formal training, individuals in the design field must be creative, imaginative, persistent, and able to communicate their ideas both visually and verbally. Because tastes in style and fashion can change quickly, designers need to be open to new ideas and influences. Problem-solving skills and the ability to work independently are important traits. People in this field need the self-discipline to start projects on their own, budget their time, and meet deadlines and production schedules. Business sense and sales ability are also important for those who freelance or run their own businesses.

Beginning designers usually receive on-the-job training and normally need one to three years of experience before they advance to higher-level positions. Experienced designers in large firms might advance to chief designer, design department head, or another supervisory position. Some experienced designers open their own firms.

Job Outlook

Despite projected faster-than-average employment growth, designers in most fields—with the exception of floral and furniture design—are expected to face competition for available positions because many talented individuals are attracted to careers as designers. Individuals with little or no formal education in design will find it difficult to establish and maintain a career in design unless they are both persistent and creative. However, opportunities for floral designers should be good, but be prepared for relatively low pay and limited opportunities for advancement.

Overall, the employment of designers is expected to grow as fast as the average, 10 to 20 percent, for all occupations through 2012. The demand for industrial designers will stem from continued emphasis on product quality and safety; design of new products that are easy and comfortable to use; high-technology products in medicine, transportation, and other fields; and increasing global competition among businesses. Rising demand for professional design of private homes, office spaces, restaurants and other retail establishments, and institutions that care for the rapidly growing elderly population should spur employment growth among interior designers.

The field of floral design should experience healthy growth with the addition of floral departments in many grocery and department stores. Demand for fashion, textile, and furniture designers should rise as consumers become more concerned with fashion and style. In addition to employment growth, many job openings will result from the need to replace designers who leave the field.

Salaries

Median annual income for full-time designers in commercial, industrial, set, exhibit, interior, floral, and fashion design was $45,000 in 2003.

Floral designers earned less than most types of designers. In 2004 the median salary for floral designers in the United States was $9.74, or about $19,500 per year for a full-time worker. Earnings tend to be higher for managers and for those on the East and West Coasts or in urban areas. Floral designers working in grocery stores earn slightly more, on average ($21,610), than designers working for florists ($18,950).

Commercial and industrial designers command much higher wages. The median salary in 2003 was $54,920, with the middle 50 percent earning between $38,630 and $68,470.

Industrial designers in managerial or executive positions earned substantially more—up to $140,000 annually. Median salaries in 2003 for other specialties were:

Set/exhibit designers	$39,070
Interior designers	$44,480
Fashion designers	$62,650

Meet Some Designers

Sara Gast, Floral Designer

Sara Gast is a self-employed floral designer from Bloomington, New York. She received her bachelor of fine arts in ceramics from SUNY–New Paltz in New York. After working as a floral designer at Mohonk Mountain House in New Paltz for a few years, she decided to work as a freelance floral designer.

"After burning out as a potter, I decided that I wanted to work with plants," she says. "And the good news was that I excelled at it. This is due in part to the fact that I so enjoyed this kind of work because of the potential to combine three important factors—working with plants, gardening, and creating artwork.

"My first floral designer job at Mohonk helped a lot. They have fabulous gardens and a hotel to decorate with flowers. In fact, later I won a 'Best of Show' award at the International Flower Show. This included a trip to Holland!

"Now I do weddings and parties and love every minute of it. We make everything for weddings—flowers for the wedding party, decorations for the church, and centerpieces, buffet displays, and cake decorations for the reception. Sometimes I have no work; sometimes I have tons. I go to the flower market in New York City at 4 A.M. on Wednesdays to begin my week. My employee is my close friend whom I trained. We are a great team.

"When we are in the process of setting up jobs, we are quite busy. And some weekends, we have up to three or four events to handle. We know we are going to spend full days on these projects: usually 9 A.M. to 5 P.M.

"I put the pressure on myself to make everything as perfect as it can be. The atmosphere is what we make it, and usually it's pretty pleasant.

"There are many things about this career that I love. I enjoy being my own boss, being able to turn down jobs I don't want to do, working with and for people I like, and getting paid to make my 'art.' I also love the compliments I receive!

"On the other hand, I don't like not having any work for long periods of time, then having tons all at once. A bit more regular spread out of events would be great, but not possible! I don't like making corsages very much; of course, there are some things I like to make more or less than others.

"I would advise those considering flower design to live in an area where there is a demand for what you do and not a glut of others already doing it. In any case, it is not a way to get rich. If you want that, go to law school or something else. I do it mostly because I love it, and I find it a challenge to realize someone's dream of what they want. So far, so good!"

Jeff Smoler, Lighting Consultant

"I have always been creative and attracted to the arts," says Jeff Smoler, a certified residential lighting consultant who also does interior and furniture design. "However, I am just as attracted to technology and have taught all phases of design and CAD."

Smoler holds both bachelor in fine arts and master of fine arts degrees. He attended the Chicago Academy of Fine Art and the University of Illinois. He also has plenty of practical experience in the areas of furniture and interior design.

"I worked my way through college as a retail furniture store chain manager and buyer," Smoler says. "Today, there is no such thing as a typical day. I work eighteen-hour days when needed. I take no lunches, and weekends and holidays sometimes elude me. Most days are hectic, since I start checking my e-mail at 6:45 A.M. each morning and finish working at 11 P.M.

"I never miss a deadline or a budget. I feel that they are set in stone. My word is something I want my clients to always be able to rely on. Being honest with my clients and my staff is foremost in my mind.

"Problem-solving is really what we do. I like the challenge of coming up with innovative design solutions on a daily basis. I dislike the paper chase and calling and calling suppliers on my clients' behalf.

"My advice to someone just starting out is to get all the education you can, join a professional organization such as ASID, get involved, strive to do your best work all the time, and be honest!"

Timothy Thoelecke, Landscape Designer

"When I came home for Christmas during my second year of college at Duke University, my parents had arranged for me to take a series of career tests," says Timothy Thoelecke, president and owner of Garden Concepts of Glenview. "The results showed that my interests and abilities were similar to those of people who were involved in design. So I came into this field from a design perspective rather than from a focus on horticulture.

"After taking the battery of career tests, I wanted to switch from my original major in English at Duke. Since there was no landscape design curriculum, I created my own program, which was heavily scrutinized and finally approved. As a result, I obtained a degree in landscape design.

"After graduating, I studied in England for a year, where I gained substantial hands-on experience. Returning to the United States, I looked around but didn't find a job that I thought would best suit me, so I put up a shingle and started my own.

"The company handles both large and small projects, ranging from a new brick patio to a new shopping center. I don't take very large projects too often because I don't want to neglect the people I deal with on a residential level. The services I provide tend to be more personal and on a one-to-one, primarily residential, level.

"The company also handles hardscape projects such as paving, sidewalks, patios, driveways, decks, lighting, and sprinkler systems—about anything anyone might want.

"I do have some specialties, though. For instance, I know a lot about perennials because of my time spent in England. . . . I know how to design with them, which is a much more difficult, time-consuming task. But this is one of the reasons I think people come to me—to get that special 'not-off-the-rack' look for their gardens and landscapes.

"Once the design work is done, we can work with clients in several ways. Some people are 'do-it-yourselfers,' so we design the project to their abilities and how much effort they are willing to expend. We outline everything that needs to be done, so it's pretty much like paint by number—though it can be back-breaking to paint by number!

"Typically we take charge of the installation all the way through, and that pretty much ensures that it will be installed the way it was designed. Then, if we run into some unfortunate things, as we inevitably do, I can be there to make on-site adjustments. Rather than having my own crews of workers, I subcontract the work out. If the project is a big job, we'll bid it out to get the best price, and the client will only have to deal with me rather than the paving, irrigating, or planting workers separately. Most of the time, I will choose a contractor I'm comfortable working with and who is best suited to the size and type of the job.

"I also do some consulting work based not only upon design but also on maintenance. Observing that some of my design projects were not looking as they should a few years down the road, and attributing this to improper maintenance, I wrote a book called *From the Ground Up*, which explains all of the things that are important in taking care of the landscape. For this effort, I am pleased to report that I was given a merit award for communications by the Illinois chapter of the American Society of Landscape Architects.

"I have a part-time administrative assistant who comes in four days a week from 9 A.M. until noon. That's really a big help to me. She answers phones, makes sure the invoices go out, inputs information into the computer, performs other office-related duties, and locates me on a job site when necessary.

"I am in the office anywhere from 6 A.M. to 8 A.M. each morning depending on the time of year and what projects are in progress. I spend a good part of the morning reading, making phone calls, following up, wrapping up paperwork—performing duties that require the capabilities of the left side of my brain. I find it's easier to switch from these kinds of activities, where I need to use logical skills, to the creative right side of the brain, rather than switching from the creative side to the logical side.

"If we have construction projects going on, I will go out to the job site, meet with owners and contractors, and make sure they are set for the day. I take a very active role during all aspects of the projects, laying out the proper places for everything from the sidewalks to the planting beds to the irrigation. My goal is to provide a landscape that is suitable for the client's lifestyle. If they really like gardening, then I'll give them certain kinds of plants. If they don't really enjoy gardening, I would choose flowers and plants that don't require a great deal of maintenance.

"If I'm lucky, I'll squeeze in a five-minute lunch while I'm reading the mail. The afternoon might bring more visits to job sites, but after that or right after lunch, if I don't have to go out to any sites, I normally spend my time at my drafting board drawing. That's when I go off into space and only come back to earth once in a while when the phone rings.

"Evenings and Saturdays, I set up appointments with clients and prospective clients. When you are self-employed, you work many hours and must handle everything from business matters to sales to marketing to creative endeavors to taking out the trash.

"A very wise, experienced nurseryman once told me that the most important thing was to 'learn your plants,' and I agree with that. There are a lot of people out there who know only a handful of plants and really don't even know where they are best suited.

"If you are interested in design, I would recommend that you learn that from a designer—not a plantsman. Design has certain principles that hold true no matter what you are designing, whether it's a pencil sharpener or the interior of a building or a landscape. In fact, the principles I learned as an English major in writing a paragraph hold true in designing a landscape. Structure, balance, and other elements have a similar relationship in all of the arts.

"I think the best part is going back to a landscape I've designed a year or two later when the plants have filled in. I absorb the look, take pictures, add them to my portfolio. It's most rewarding to enjoy the fulfillment of seeing something completed, something tangible, something beautiful—something I've helped to create."

Chari Hendricks, Floral Designer

"I attended Mundelein College and completed the program for associates in design," says Chari Hendricks, floral designer and owner of the Flower Petal in Illinois. "Flowers were always a passion for me, so I combined my design background with this love and made floral design my career. I've been involved in this endeavor for more than ten years.

"You must be able to make people with varying tastes happy. Although I have my own likes and dislikes, my aim is to create something that my client will enjoy. It really doesn't matter whether I personally love it.

"It is my job to create fresh, dried, and silk flower arrangements. I'm very picky about the freshness of flowers and usually take them in on a daily basis to use for that day and the next. It's important to create beautiful designs, but if the flowers die rapidly, you are not going to keep that person as a customer. Sometimes, though, I make an arrangement with the idea of its drying. It can then be enjoyed even after it has died. I always choose the containers carefully because they are an important part of the presentation.

"It's always a challenge to know what flowers to have on hand and how much to order. Each geographic location is different because people are often different from one area to another. But once you've done this kind of work for a while, you get to know. People tell you directly what they like and what they don't like. You must also keep in mind the time of the year, because certain flowers sell better at specific times.

"I buy from a combination of wholesale florists, and I also wholesale dried products to others. Beyond this, I use nurseries that grow their own blooming plants (rather than those that import them) because then I am sure they know if something is wrong with them. For instance, the plants could have bugs.

"One thing that is very important is to give people their money's worth. Whether it's a $25 arrangement or a $200 arrangement, time should be properly put in to make that creation something special.

"I go to people's homes, especially for the dried arrangements or when a client needs a lot. Often they want me to see the setting, and it's quite valuable for me to avoid guesswork. I might also want to get a close look at the surroundings when involved in creating a party centerpiece, for example. Of course, we do weddings and funerals and provide flowers and plants for all occasions.

"You must really know what you're dealing with—names of flowers, how to care for them, colors. Some schools are good at teaching this, and some are not. As a student, though, it's your fault if you are not properly prepared. If you see you are not getting this information, you should study on your own to pick up this knowledge. If they're not teaching you, you owe it to yourself to teach yourself. There are many markets you can go to and books to consult to familiarize yourself with the different flowers.

"In my career it's important to be flexible. The amount of business goes up and down very rapidly depending on the season of the year. You have to enjoy the quiet times to help you get through the more stressful times. Christmas can get pretty tense. Additionally, you never know which days are going to be busy and which are going to be quiet. And you have to be prepared for either one.

"You also have to be willing to do some 'grunt' work. Even someone with a degree will probably not design immediately. Regardless, there are always flowers that need cleaning, floors that need to be swept, plants that need watering. You must learn how to properly wrap a package. Not all of the work is glamorous; you can't have a 'prima donna' attitude if you want to be successful.

"Flower design can be both intrinsically and financially rewarding. If you're just starting, you can expect $7 to $8 an hour. But I think most good designers who have experience expect a minimum of $35,000 a year. Remember, a good designer can make or break a store. Owners are usually happy to pay those who will bring in business."

Enrico Manfredini, Landscape Designer

"I was literally born into this line of work," says Enrico Manfredini of Manfredini Landscaping and Design, based in Illinois. "My father founded the company almost thirty years ago, and I have always been around it and involved in it. From the time I was able, I spent summers and whatever time I had helping out and pitching in. My formal education consists of a certificate in ornamental horticulture from College of Lake County in Illinois.

"I learned a lot at school—the basics of botanical names, plant identification, plant diseases, and the proper techniques for planting and maintenance. In addition, I gained a tremendous amount of knowledge from my father and from applying common sense. But I'd have to say that my on-the-job experience was probably most important. In this business, you must learn quickly because mistakes are costly. So when you're out there, you learn quickly.

"The company employs forty people. We have fifteen trucks and various machinery and equipment, which we service ourselves. Our client list numbers approximately three hundred, who are serviced weekly. Of course, new jobs come up at regular intervals, and many involve design and implementation with or without regular maintenance afterward.

"We handle every aspect of landscaping, working hand in hand with landscape architects. This might involve designing and installing decks, walks, and patios or setting up irrigation, sprinkling, or lighting systems. Our services run the gamut from planting large thirty-foot trees to installing small perennial rock gardens with waterfalls and ponds. Much of our focus is on our weekly clients, who subscribe to our regular maintenance service. This requires mowing lawns, trimming shrubs, and eliminating insects. This last one requires licensing by the state of Illinois and must be recertified every three years.

"We have performed a substantial amount of work for municipal clients in the area, such as school districts, libraries, parks, and cities or villages themselves. Recently, for instance, we planted five hundred trees for the village of Highland Park.

"We also handle some special projects that are quite spectacular. The most prominent that comes to mind is a three-acre estate that we completely renovated. This included putting in irrigation systems, lighting, a redesigned driveway, a fourteen-foot round fountain with a ram's head that spews water, formal rose gardens, bluestone patios, and crushed bluestone walkways that are lit up. To add privacy, we planted evergreens, deciduous shrubs, and flowering trees.

"In another area, we developed a large vegetable garden, approximately one hundred feet long by thirty feet wide. It's all enclosed with decorative fencing and other unusual features like arches. Next year we will continue our work by adding a meadow and some perennial gardens. It's all quite breathtaking!

"Even though I found my on-the-job experience so valuable, I would still recommend to others that they continue their schooling and get a landscape architecture degree. If I had acquired a landscape architecture degree, I would have complete control over projects and be able to complete all the work, instead of having to hire a landscape architect. This, of course, would be personally and financially beneficial. I can and do perform design work, but some doors are closed to me because I don't have this credential.

"I would heartily encourage others to enter this career, as I have found it to be extremely rewarding and satisfying."

Professional Associations

For a list of accredited schools of art and design, contact:

National Association of Schools of Art and Design
11250 Roger Bacon Drive, Suite 21
Reston, VA 20190
http://nasad.arts-accredit.org

For information on careers and a list of academic programs in industrial design, write to:

Industrial Designers Society of America
45195 Business Court, Suite 250
Dulles, VA 20166
www.idsa.org

For information on degrees, continuing education, and licensing programs in interior design, contact:

American Society for Interior Designers
608 Massachusetts Avenue NE
Washington, DC 20002
www.asid.org

For a list of accredited programs in interior design, contact:

Foundation for Interior Design Education Research
146 Monroe Center NW, Suite 1318
Grand Rapids, MI 49503
www.fider.org

For information about careers in floral design, contact:

Society of American Florists
1601 Duke Street
Alexandria, VA 22314
www.safnow.org

For a list of schools with accredited programs in furniture design, contact:

American Society of Furniture Designers
144 Woodland Drive
New London, NC 28127
www.asfd.com

CHAPTER THREE

Studio Artists

Art is the most intense mode of individualism
that the world has known.
—Oscar Wilde

Your love of color, coupled with your artistic talent and skill, has led you toward a career as a practicing artist. Your goal is to be able to create works of art that allow for self-expression and the need to make a living. Perhaps you even long to open your own studio, a place in which to create and sell your own work. Whether it's pottery or painting, sewing or stained glass, it is possible for artists and artisans to make a name for themselves and work full-time in their chosen areas—without starving in the proverbial artist's garret.

Having said that, few studio artists can move immediately into a career that provides adequate financial support, at least at first. It takes time to build a reputation or a clientele, and during those "lean years," many artists seek out additional employment so they can be assured of a regular paycheck. The other chapters in this book cover related careers that you can consider pursuing while you're establishing yourself.

But whether you're moonlighting in other areas or are able to devote yourself entirely to your art, you probably have some questions about the different forms of studio art and the options for employment. Let's take a look at the possibilities available to color connoisseurs.

A Look at Studio Art Disciplines

Painting

Painters generally work on canvas, producing two-dimensional art forms, although they are not restricted to this alone. Some paint on furniture or clothing. Others specialize in large wall murals. The surfaces painters can use are limited only by their imaginations.

Painters study and use the techniques of shading, perspective, and color mixing. They may produce works that portray realistic scenes, or they might choose to work with more abstract depictions, evoking different moods and emotions. The materials they use include oils, watercolors, acrylics, pastels, magic markers, pencils, pen and ink, and charcoal.

Sculpture

Sculptors work with three-dimensional art forms, either molding and joining materials—such as clay, glass, wire, plastic, or metal—or cutting and carving forms from a block of plaster, wood, stone, or even ice. Some sculptors combine materials such as concrete, metal, wood, plastic, and paper.

Pottery

Potters work with a variety of clays—from low-fire clays to high-fire stoneware or porcelain—and either hand build their art work or create forms using a potter's wheel. Those using the wheel have the choice of electric wheels or kick wheels.

Some potters might work in production pottery, turning out large numbers of the same item. Others spend their time making one-of-a-kind pieces.

In every case, potters dry and trim their pieces, fire them, then glaze them for final firing. They follow existing glaze recipes or experiment with different chemicals to formulate their own.

Printmaking

Printmakers create printed images on fabric, paper, or other media. They use designs cut into wood, stone, or metal or from computer-driven data. The designs might be engraved, as in the case of woodblocking; etched, as in the production of etchings; or derived from computers in the form of ink-jet or laser prints.

Stained Glass

Stained-glass artists work with glass, paint, lead, wood, and other materials to create functional as well as decorative artwork, such as windows, skylights, and doors. They repair existing stained-glass windows and produce new designs.

Photography

Photographers use a variety of equipment when making photographs, including cameras, lenses, film, filters, tripods, flashes, and light meters. Those who develop their own prints in the darkroom use chemicals and paper—in much the same way a painter uses paint and canvas. They capture realistic scenes of people, places, and events or make abstract images using special effects.

Woodworking

Woodworkers create furniture and accessories such as jewelry boxes, bowls, and picture frames. The saying goes that woodworkers are only as good as their tools. Some choose to work with only hand tools, such as planes and chisels. Others stock their workshops with a full array of power tools, including table saws, jointers, and sanders. They also use a variety of oils, paints, stains, and varnishes.

Other Crafts

Other art and craft forms, including needlepoint, crewel, quilting, rug making, papier-mâché, tole, basketry, and doll making. Artisans work with a wide variety of materials in producing their art.

Job Settings

Studios and Storefronts

Studio artists generally work in art and design studios located in commercial spaces or in their own homes. Some artists prefer to work alone; others require the stimulation of other artists working nearby. For them, sharing space with other artists is often a viable alternative to the lone studio—both for stimulation and for economic reasons, since shared space costs less money. In many large cities and even smaller towns, artists share space in cooperatively owned studios or in rented warehouses or storefronts that have been converted for their specific needs.

Artists with their own or shared space often have storefronts in which to sell their work. Artists might also depend on stores, museums, corporate collections, art galleries, and private homes as outlets for their work. Some work might be done on request from clients; other works are made "on spec" before the artist finds interested buyers.

Art Fairs

Some artists follow the art-fair or craft-fair circuits, touring the country on a regular basis, deriving most, if not all, of their income from this source alone. However, many artists will tell you that this option can be risky, with no guarantee of sales. In addition, the fair circuit is vulnerable to changes in weather and the whims of impulse buyers or true art lovers and collectors.

Mail Order

There are publications that cater to almost every craft, from doll collecting to antique quilt restoration. Many artisans are familiar with the magazines that are geared toward their craft. There they can find a home to advertise their products to a targeted audience of collectors.

Living-History Museums

Most living-history museums employ skilled artisans—potters, silversmiths, wig makers, needleworkers, costumers, woodworkers, candle makers, blacksmiths, to name just a few—to demonstrate early crafts and trades. Some of these artisans perform their art while playing the role of a particular character from the time. Others wear twentieth-century clothing and discuss their craft from a modern perspective.

In addition to demonstrations, artisans often produce many of the items used on display in the various exhibits or for sale in the museum gift shops. These include furniture, cookware, and sometimes actual buildings. Colonial Williamsburg in Williamsburg, Virginia, and Plimoth Plantation in Plymouth, Massachusetts, are just two examples of living-history museums.

Training and Qualifications

In the fine-arts field, your talent speaks for you, and there are no real formal training requirements. But it is very difficult to become skilled enough to make a living without some basic training. Bachelor's and graduate degree programs in fine arts are offered at many colleges and universities (see the Appendix).

In addition to the skills learned or honed, those studying in colleges or art schools make important contacts during their formal training years. Instructors are often working artists with hands-on experience and advice to offer.

Competition

The fine-arts field has a glamorous and exciting image. Many people with creative ability pursue a livelihood in the various sectors of this field. As a result, there is always keen competition for both salaried employment and freelance work.

However, employment of fine artists is expected to grow because of population growth, rising incomes, and growth in the number of people who appreciate fine arts. Graphic arts studios, clients, and galleries alike are always on the lookout for artists who display outstanding talent, creativity, and style. Talented artists who have developed a mastery of artistic techniques and skills should continue to be in great demand.

Salaries

As any artist knows, the money doesn't come in regularly, but for those who are persistent, there is money to be made. Sometimes it comes in big chunks; thus, it is important to learn how to budget so the money carries you through the leaner times.

Earnings for self-employed visual artists vary widely. Those struggling to gain experience and a reputation might be forced to charge what amounts to less than the minimum wage for their work. Well-established artists may earn much more than salaried artists, although self-employed artists do not receive benefits, such as paid holidays, sick leave, health insurance, or pensions.

When starting your own studio, you can set things up slowly. A new artist usually can't afford state-of-the-art equipment. Buying secondhand equipment and building your own workbenches and furniture will lower your start-up costs.

Artists who are lucky to land shows with galleries usually determine with the gallery owner in advance how much each will earn from a sale. Only the most successful fine artists are able to support themselves solely through sale of their work, however.

Meet Some Studio Artists

Howard Wexler, Photographer

"I first became interested in still photography, and later in cinematography, after watching Hollywood movies," says Howard

Wexler, a California freelance director of photography. Wexler graduated from the University of Southern California Division of Cinema. "My early work involved shooting high school football games and short films for friends," Wexler says. "Since then I have shot over forty features as director of photography and many other film and video shoots as operator, second unit, and aerial specialist. I like telling a story visually and really enjoy films that tell a story with a minimum of words.

"To secure work, I send out lots of resumes and VHS reels of my work that I have compiled into a seven-minute demo. Then I usually follow up with a phone call and sometimes get an interview. I 'pitch' myself and ask to read the script or meet the director. Hopefully there is something in the material or personalities involved that attracts me to the projects, and if all goes well, I am offered a job.

"If I get the job, I carefully reread the script, make a list of crew and equipment I think it will take to shoot the film, and meet again with the producer or production coordinator.

"For budget reasons, my list is usually trimmed down, and then we make more lists and phone calls to line up the crew I want to work with. Then we scout the locations, talk over the look of the visuals and lighting, and plan to get the most out of our days.

"On the set, I direct the crew to place the camera and lights. I operate the camera myself, with the help of an assistant who keeps the lens in focus. The gaffer and I confer about the lighting, and the key grip helps in positioning the camera. We usually work twelve to fourteen hours a day, most of the time on our feet. You really have to love the work to stay in it!

"Lunch is scheduled for six hours after we start, and sometimes we have another meal six hours later. We drink plenty of water and eat snacks throughout the day or night. Sometimes there are many other crew members—sometimes I do everything all by myself.

"There can be danger in this job. In the past, I have sometimes hung out of airplanes or helicopters to get just the shot the director wants. I just trust the [pilot] and make sure I'm strapped in. I have been to some places few people get to and have seen sights few people have. Every day is different, which makes for an exciting time, with new people to make as friends and creative challenges on every job.

"The most important thing to getting into this line of work is to watch the light wherever you go, follow the sun every day of the year, and watch shadows, too! Shoot stills with any still camera to develop your eye to be discriminating, with an attention to detail and nuances of movement. Speed reading helps to improve your eye muscles. The simple method of looking through an empty toilet paper tube can make you aware of what a 50 mm lens is and how you can give the audience just certain information. It all comes down to story, however, and what the message or entertainment value of the time spent in viewing the material is. A director of photography can help make a film enjoyable and entertaining to watch."

Bob Campagna, Photographer

"About twenty years ago, I had a visual awakening and began teaching myself photography," Bob Campagna says. "I had not previously taken an art course, but I began to feel a need to be artistic, and photography became the tool of love and choice. Today, I am a photographer, an educator, and the owner of my own business.

"I was attracted to photography because it blended many disciplines, including art, visualization, math, chemistry, English, social studies, and history, among others. To me, each photograph became the balance point of these disciplines. With photography I could not only have direct control over my own involvements and travels but could also use the gift of photography for larger purposes. In this respect, I donate much of my time toward photography education as well as photographing for political and educational purposes.

"The bottom line for me is that photography is a tool that enables me to have a vision and make that vision come true.

"In college I studied English and received a bachelor of arts degree from the University of Iowa. However, I feel that writing is often too personal and hence not commercial. By incorporating photography into my pursuits, I was able to blend text and pictures, and this opened the doors to becoming a photojournalist, which I did for two years at a newspaper. Photography evolved chiefly because there was a vacancy in my work life, a gap, and the act of being an artist filled that gap. Otherwise I would have just continued to work for the purpose of money.

"Every day is a challenge to find new people to connect with, to make a collective vision. Also, I need to let go of the people with whom the vision has ended. Each day differs. Some days are spent teaching through the Iowa Arts Council. Others are spent in the darkroom producing images. Others are spent photographing on location for specific projects. Others are spent watching my children's involvements in music, theater, and athletics. Others are spent walking the land. And more.

"This kind of work can be busy, relaxed, or dangerous. All elements are possible and have occurred. Dangerous includes having photographed in a war zone in Nicaragua or in places that are physically dangerous, such as abandoned houses or grain elevators.

"Work can consume a week, but probably sixty hours would be typical. Sometimes teaching residencies require fifteen-hour days, and then some. However, since I work from home, my schedule is very flexible and can be stopped when needed. I have a professional studio that is spacious, efficient, and welcoming to a visitor.

"On the positive side, this career offers the chance to be a creator and visionary and to associate with kindred spirits. On the negative side, it requires collecting money and paying bills.

"Being self-employed is a matter of having your own dream and working for your own dream. However, to work for yourself means there is no slack time. You must always be aware. You can't call in sick and get paid or hide from the boss. But what you end up doing is the direct result of the dreams you have. Certainly this can also happen in other places of employment, but being a self-employed artist means that you have no place to hide and no guarantees about anything other than once you embark on this lifestyle, you will never be able to retire. You will always be an artist."

Debra Moss, Photographer

"I always enjoyed photography as a hobby," says Debra Moss, a Florida freelance photographer and writer, "so I decided to turn it into a career. I worked as a freelance contract archeologist surveyor for five years in Florida, Georgia, and the U.S. Virgin Islands after receiving my master of arts degree in archeology from Ohio State University in Columbus. In 1987, I became a freelance photographer while living in the Virgin Islands. I covered Caribbean travel, yachting, and sailing regattas.

"Then I began searching for a way to add creativity and soul to my life, so I built a portfolio and started sending it out to magazines, hoping to sell my work. Several editors called me and said they loved my photos, but could I write something to go with it? I have always loved writing, so I gave it a shot. Soon I was specializing in selling text/photo packages to magazines. I now have over 150 published credits, including some very well-respected ones such as *Outside*, *Bicycling*, *Yachting*, and many others. I penned columns on computer use for writers, historical and architectural photography, and how to shoot sailboat races and others action sports. I was the press liaison for the internationally known America's Paradise Triathlon on St. Croix.

"My technique is somewhat unique—I use only natural light and have never owned a flash system, so all my work is done outdoors. I try to capture only beauty and have never gone in for what I call the somber side of the profession, photography noir.

"Travel photography, in particular, has allowed me to travel to many places on a magazine's budget. This has probably been the greatest lure. For example, this past March a magazine sent me to Costa Rica to shoot and write an article on surfing. Since I am a surfer, this was quite an enticing offer—and much fun. I love my work, and people are always stunned by the way my camera sees things.

"I took a creative writing class once, but I have no formal education in [writing], nor have I ever even taken a photography course. I am told I have 'an eye,' which I believe is an innate ability to see the world in a specific way. (I learned this from a famous photographer who looked at my work and said exactly that—'Well, you certainly have the eye.') After that, it's mostly a matter of learning the mechanics of light, shutters, and lens—the tools of the trade.

"In six years of college, I learned that anything you could ever want to know is in books, so I read every photography book I could find, then went out and shot a hundred rolls of film. That was the sum total of my training.

"Every day is a completely new experience. I don't photograph every day because I work on assignment, but I do write every day. I occasionally go out and shoot for fun so as not to lose sight of the joy I used to feel when I did it only for me and not a paying customer. My husband works at night, and I only shoot in the day, so sometimes he comes with me and carries my equipment. He is not taken in by the art of what I do particularly, but he enjoys watching me work and going to the places it takes me. I am now living near the ocean outside Jacksonville, Florida, and have done numerous articles and photos on Amelia Island for *Ritz Carlton* magazine. Next week I will be taking the ferry to Cumberland Island to interview and photograph the great-granddaughter of Thomas Carnegie.

"In a normal week, I work about five hours a day, five days a week. The rest of the time I train for triathlons and surf. Not a bad life.

"What bothered me most at first was my insecurity. I hadn't proven to myself that I had earned the right to represent myself as 'a photographer.' My first assignment was scary, as I was expected to produce what someone else wanted, and what if I couldn't, or my camera broke, or it rained? It was nerve-wracking, and I don't like stress much, but over the years I have learned what I can do, what I am pretty good at, and what I can do that hardly anyone else can. That self-knowledge of specialty has taken the stress away.

"Also, the uncertainty of payment when you freelance almost requires you have a steady backup income (a spouse or trust fund is nice) or at least a nest egg so that you can go for six months without seeing a dime to get you through until that blissful day when ten [payments] arrive in the mail together. Other than that, I think being a photographer is just about the neatest profession there is.

"I would recommend that you read everything there is to read, take your camera everywhere you go, and let your camera take you places you would never have gone."

Carol Revzan, Weaver

"I love to make things," says Carol Revzan, a weaver and yarn business owner from Evanston, Illinois. "And it all started when my grandmother taught me to knit and crochet many years ago. After I had been doing so for many years, I saw an antique coverlet, and I knew I had to learn to weave. Several years later, I found a teacher and started weaving.

"Taking a strand of yarn and manipulating it into fabric or clothing is endlessly fascinating," Revzan says. "The combinations of color, texture, and weave structures possible ensure that I shall never be at a loss for what to do next! Since 1964, I have never been without a project involving yarn or thread. I also love selling yarn and helping people find just that right yarn for their next project.

"I have my studio in my home and work alone. A typical workday starts about 9 A.M. and involves weaving until noon, with more weaving after lunch. Later in the afternoon, I work on finishing past projects or planning new ones. A good bit of time is required to design and plan a project before yarn can be threaded onto the loom. I also host once-a-month weaving classes and always have time for anyone to stop by and purchase yarn.

"What I like most is being able to set my own schedule, develop designs and projects, and have time to continue to learn and stretch myself creatively. And do I love taking finished cloth off the loom!

"What I like least is the fact that this kind of work is a bit lonely at times and that it's hard to get a good financial return for the time and effort put into handwoven things.

"I would tell others that good weaving techniques are essential and that a background in color theory and art is most helpful. Though it's difficult to make a living at it, combined with other activities, it can be very rewarding."

David Klobucar, Photojournalist

"I grew up in Kansas City and attended Oak Park High School," David Klobucar, an editor and photojournalist for the *Chicago Tribune*, says. "In my junior year, I took a camera course and found I was really interested in photography. So I signed up for the yearbook course and became the photographer for the yearbook, which developed my interests even further. After graduation I attended the University of Missouri at Columbia as a biochemistry major, but after a year I knew that I was going to have problems with classes such as calculus. Discovering that the university had an excellent journalism program, I switched to my second love and earned a bachelor's degree in journalism with a major in photography.

"For the next ten years, I accepted positions in Jackson, Mississippi; Omaha, Nebraska; and Springfield, Illinois. I was doing freelance work and becoming somewhat disillusioned with the newspaper industry when my wife was offered a good position in Chicago, and we moved there. After about six months, I received a call from the *Chicago Tribune* asking me to work part-time. I did so for a year and a half until they asked me to become a full-time employee. It's funny—when I left Springfield, I had no intention of going back into newspaper work, but I realized that though there were some things I didn't like about it, there were many more that I did.

"A typical week in the life of a photojournalist is probably a lot less exciting than people think. The day is broken into shifts from 7 A.M. until 11 or 12 at night, with photojournalists putting in eight-hour shifts. About thirty to forty-five minutes before my shift is supposed to start, I call in and find out if they have anything special for me to do. If they don't have any specific assignments for me that day, they tell me what general area of the city they want me in, and I start driving into that area. If two photojournalists are assigned to one area, we head in opposite directions so that we have the area fully covered. I have two scanners in my car and a company radio, so if my office needs to get ahold of me, they can contact me at any time with an assignment. Or if I hear something on the scanner that I think might be interesting, I might check into it.

"We split the day between taking photographs and getting them ready for publication. If I were working a shift that started at 9 A.M., for example, I would stay out in the field until 2 or 3 P.M., then come back to the office to process which frames I want used and submit them to the picture editor. Since we don't make prints anymore—everything is electronic—I upload the image into a computer, attach the image to a caption and [put it in] a slot that tells which story it goes with.

"If I come across any good stories that interest me, I can develop my own projects. For instance, a reporter and I were out at the Chicago Housing Authority one day talking with some security people. It occurred to me that these guards could form the basis of a great story profiling a new program recently launched there. The reporter and I subsequently pitched the idea by making a proposal and turning it in to our editor. If it's decided that the story is worthwhile, the reporter and I will continue our efforts. I prefer to work this way, because the images and the words tend to match a lot better if you're both seeing the same thing. If you don't work as a team, you're not telling the same story.

"In order to be a successful photojournalist, you must be a self-starter. If you don't take the initiative to seek out how it all fits together, you will not succeed. You need to have curiosity about the world, about people, and about photojournalism. With the vision of a psychologist, you must be able to read people in order to help them understand what you're trying to do. A lot of people are very suspicious of what you are doing, but really you're simply trying to understand their world.

"You always need to remember that you are trying to be a visual communicator. The images need to be thoughtful and compelling in terms of composition, movement, lighting. It's not just walking into a situation, clicking the shutter, and walking away.

"A lot of people think photojournalism is really easy and fun. Admittedly, this is a very interesting career, but it's also very demanding. There are a number of skills that you must bring to the job in order to produce exciting images. You don't use one skill at a time; you must have a bagful of skills at your disposal at all times."

Dave Knoderer, Artist

Dave Knoderer is a self-employed artist based in Sarasota, Florida. His artistic nickname is "Letterfly." He attended the University of Southern Illinois at Carbondale and then worked as an artist apprentice for several years. He keeps up with his education by attending several annual workshops and maintaining memberships in several art-related associations. His marketing materials describe him this way: "Letterfly is the top producer of the high-quality airbrushed murals seen on the outsides of luxury motor homes. Wildlife and animal depictions provide the mainstay for these works. In addition to paintwork on the exterior of motor homes, the artist also produces mural work found in homes and oil paintings on canvas."

"As a child, I was encouraged to create," Knoderer says. "And painting and exhibit building are natural for me. I was attracted to the profession by the ability to provide a service to almost anyone (at the beginning) in about any location. I enjoyed the freedom to be creative and explore this wonderful land of ours and provide a service to everyone.

"The most fulfilling part of my job is experiencing the magnitude of joy that my customers have as the result of my completing a painting for them. Many times it is a genuine honor for me to be painting something for these special people. My love of my fellow man coupled with sharing my gift with them is very fulfilling.

"How many hours a week? The early career days were typically spent being creative. As my ability developed, I found that in order to reach another audience (one that would appreciate the level I had achieved), I had to be involved in more and more marketing. Today I spend about a quarter of my time just communicating with people and writing stories and getting publicity in the right places and less and less time (it seems) behind a brush. When I do work, I am focused, and I pour all I have into the project. Perhaps the new blend of investing my time is better for the diversification of creation.

"Thanks to my itinerant lifestyle, every job is like an adventure. I never know if I am going to have to trudge through the mud at a current construction site to get to work on the mural I have been commissioned to do, or if I have been provided with a spacious shop to begin the project in the midst of luxury.

"The creative energy I have is satisfied when I am asked for my ideas. It seems that of all I do, it is the having of ideas that elevates me above my peers and makes me a person in demand. Oddly enough, the having of ideas isn't what earns any money; it is only after the idea is presented as a plan and executed as a finished work that it realizes any income.

"The being itinerant is good in that it allows me to be very selective about the jobs I want to do, and that has a lot to do with the success I have enjoyed. The bad side is that I do not have the permanence in the community I desire, and I have no family. I am sure that when I meet my soul mate, it will be time to make some appropriate changes, and then I will choose to travel less.

"Tremendous sacrifice is what it took for me to get to the level of ability that I enjoy today. Dedication and perspiration are also essential ingredients. The becoming and the ability to give of this wonderful gift have always been paramount. Perhaps the most despised part of the business of being an artist is the business end of it all. I was very naïve, and as a result of that, I was taken advantage of in the early stages of my career. Potential and practicing artists should be aware that a strong business head would be a tremendous asset."

Professional Associations

American Arts Alliance
1112 Sixteenth Street NW, Suite 400
Washington, DC 20036
www.amercanartsalliance.org

American Craft Council
72 Spring Street
New York, NY 10012
www.craftcouncil.org

American Society of Interior Designers
608 Massachusetts Avenue NE
Washington, DC 20002
www.asid.org

Americans for the Arts
(Washington, DC, office)
1000 Vermont Avenue NW, Sixth Floor
Washington, DC 20005

Americans for the Arts
(New York office)
One East Fifty-third Street
New York, NY 10022
www.artsusa.org

National Museum of American History
Smithsonian Institution
PO Box 37012
Fourteenth Street and Constitution Avenue
Washington, DC 20004
http://americanhistory.si.edu

Costume Society of America
55 Edgewater Drive
PO Box 73
Earleville, MD 21919
www.costumesocietyamerica.com

National Association of Schools of Art and Design
11250 Roger Bacon Drive, Suite 21
Reston, VA 20190
http://nasad.arts-accredit.org

National Assembly of State Arts Agencies
1029 Vermont Avenue NW, Second Floor
Washington, DC 20005
www.nasaa-arts.org

CHAPTER FOUR

Commercial Artists

Anyone who says you can't see a thought simply doesn't know art.
—Wynetka Ann Reynolds

The lifestyle of employed commercial artists, also known as graphic artists and illustrators, is financially much more secure than that of studio artists. Getting that regular paycheck, however, may mean sacrificing some of the artistic freedom that studio artists enjoy. While many fine artists produce art for art's sake, graphic artists and illustrators put their artistic skills and vision at the service of commercial clients, such as major corporations, retail stores, and advertising, design, or publishing firms.

A Look at Commercial Artists

Graphic artists perform different jobs depending on their area of expertise and the needs of their employers. Some work for only one employer; others freelance and work for a variety of clients. In fact, nearly 60 percent of commercial artists are self-employed, about seven times the norm for other professional occupations.

A sampling of the career paths available for commercial artists demonstrates the range of possibilities.

Graphic Designer

Graphic designers design on a two-dimensional level. They might create packaging and promotional displays for a new product, the visual design of an annual report and other corporate literature, or a distinctive logo for a product or business. They might create graphics for television or assist with the layout and design of magazines, newspapers, journals, and other publications.

Illustrator

Illustrators paint or draw pictures for books, magazines, and other publications, as well as for films and paper products, such as greeting cards, calendars, wrapping paper, and stationery. Many do a variety of illustrations, while others specialize in a particular style.

Medical and Scientific Illustrator

Medical and scientific illustrators combine artistic skills with knowledge of the biological sciences. Medical illustrators draw illustrations of human anatomy and surgical procedures. Scientific illustrators draw illustrations of animals and plants.

These illustrations are used in medical and scientific journals and related publications and in audiovisual presentations for teaching purposes. Medical illustrators also work for lawyers, producing exhibits for court cases, and for doctors.

Fashion Artist

Fashion artists draw illustrations of women's, men's, and children's clothing and accessories for newspapers, magazines, mail-order catalogs, and other media.

Storyboard Artist

Storyboards for television commercials are also drawn by illustrators. Storyboards present TV commercials in a series of scenes similar to a comic strip so an advertising agency and client (the company doing the advertising) can evaluate the proposed commercials. Storyboards also serve as guides to placement of actors and cameras and other details during production.

Cartoonist

Cartoonists draw political, advertising, social, and sports cartoons. Some cartoonists work with others who create the idea or story and write the captions. Most cartoonists, however, have a talent for humor, critique, or drama in addition to drawing skills.

Animator

Animators work in the motion picture and television industries. They draw by hand and also use computers to create the large series of pictures that, when transferred to film or tape, form the animated cartoons seen in movies and on television.

Art Director

Art directors, also called visual journalists, read the material to be printed in periodicals, newspapers, and other printed media and decide how to visually present the information in an eye-catching yet organized manner.

Art directors make decisions about which photographs or artwork to use and in general oversee production of the printed material. Art directors might also review graphics that will be displayed online.

The Tools of the Trade

Commercial artists, whether employed by a firm or working freelance, use a variety of print, electronic, and film media to create art that meets a client's needs. Graphic artists in every discipline increasingly use computers instead of the traditional tools of design, such as pens, pencils, mat knives, and color strips, to produce their work. Computers allow them to lay out and test various designs, type styles, formats, and colors before printing a final design.

Working Conditions

Graphic artists work in art and design studios located in office buildings or their own homes. Graphic artists employed by publishing companies and art and design studios generally work a forty-hour week. During busy periods, they might work overtime to meet deadlines.

Self-employed graphic artists can set their own hours, but they usually end up working more than a standard work week. Often they find they are spending a large part of their time and effort in two areas: selling their services to potential clients and establishing a reputation.

Getting Started

A poll of established professionals elicited these helpful hints for those just starting out:

1. **Go to the best art school** possible for your formal training.
2. **Know your software.** Learn Adobe Photoshop, Adobe InDesign, Adobe Illustrator or Macromedia FreeHand, and QuarkXPress, and, if you're designing for the Web, such programs as Macromedia Dreamweaver, Flash, and Fireworks. Add to your skills as much as you can before college.
3. **Begin building your portfolio** by freelancing in college.
4. **Target the type of work you want to do.** Then study the careers of artists doing similar work.
5. **Write to other artists** to learn how they got started.
6. **Don't worry about what city you're in.** The days of big advertising design firms are gone. More and more people are working as freelancers all over the country.
7. **Be flexible.** The field changes rapidly, and your ability to change with it is important.

Job Settings

Until they get established, many graphic artists work part-time as freelancers while continuing to hold full-time jobs. Others have enough perseverance and confidence in their ability to start out freelancing full-time immediately after they graduate from art school.

The freelance artist develops a set of clients who regularly contract for work. Some successful freelancers are widely recognized for specialized skills in children's book illustration, design, or magazine illustration. These artists can earn high incomes and can pick and choose the type of work they do. But more often than not, freelance careers take time to build. While making contacts and developing skills, many find employment to make ends meet. Other commercial artists choose full-time employment over freelancing. They find work in a variety of settings.

Advertising Agencies and Design Firms

People starting out in advertising agencies or graphic design studios often begin with routine work. While doing this work, however, they can observe and practice their skills on the side. Jobs can cover anything from direct-mail packages to catalog work, posters, and even television and motion pictures.

Publishing Companies

Magazine, newspaper, and book publishers require the expertise of commercial artists for a wide range of duties, including cover design, advertising layout, typesetting, and graphics.

Department Stores

Department stores, especially the larger chains, routinely produce catalogs, direct-mail packages, flyers, posters, and a variety of other advertising and promotional materials. While small stores might send the work out to freelancers, large department stores often have fully staffed departments to handle the workload.

Television and Motion Picture Industry

With Disney's and other companies' shift to computer-generated animation for feature films, traditional cell animation has taken a huge hit. There are, however, a few studios still producing films using traditional animation if this is a vocation you're determined to pursue. There are also corresponding jobs that have opened up in computer animation, although not nearly enough to offset the loss of positions for hand illustrators.

Other settings include manufacturing firms and the various agencies within the local, state, and federal government.

Training and Qualifications

Graphic Arts

In the graphic arts field, demonstrated ability and appropriate training or other qualifications are needed to enter the field and get ahead. Successful job candidates demonstrate their talent and skill through a portfolio, which is an important factor used by art and design directors in deciding whether to hire or contract out work to an artist.

The portfolio is a collection of handmade, computer-generated, or printed examples of the artist's best work. In theory, a person with a good portfolio but no training or experience could succeed as a graphic artist. In reality, assembling a successful portfolio requires skills generally developed in a postsecondary art or design school program, such as a bachelor's degree program in fine art, graphic design, or visual communications.

Internships also provide excellent opportunities for artists and designers to develop and enhance their portfolios. Most programs in art and design also provide training in computer design techniques. This training is essential for many of the jobs found in commercial art.

Medical Illustration

The appropriate training and education for prospective medical illustrators is more specific. Medical illustrators not only must demonstrate artistic ability, they must also have a detailed knowledge of living organisms, surgical and medical procedures, and human and sometimes animal anatomy.

A four-year bachelor's degree combining art and premedical courses is usually required, followed by a master's degree in medical illustration, a degree offered in only a few accredited schools in the United States.

In general, illustrators advance as their work circulates and as they establish a reputation for a particular style. The best illustrators continue to grow in ideas, and their work evolves over time.

Strategies for the Job Hunt

As in most any professional career, contacts and a "foot in the door" at the type of organization for which you'd like to work are valuable assets. Internships are pathways to both. The best strategy is to plan ahead. During your undergraduate or graduate studies, arrange for as many internships as you can squeeze in—either full-time during the summers or part-time during semesters.

Learning how an advertising agency, a PR firm, or a TV studio functions will give you a broad overview and also help you build a successful portfolio. If an internship gave you a foot in the door, a professional and creative portfolio can open that door all the way. In addition, find yourself a mentor, someone who can critique your portfolio and advise you on how best to proceed.

Salaries

Entry-level full-time graphic designers earned a median annual salary of $30,000, according to the *AIGA/Aquent Survey of Design*

Salaries 2003. Senior designers earned a median salary of $52,000, and Web designers earned $48,000. Art directors earned a median salary of $60,000, with the seventy-fifth percentile at $75,000 and the twenty-fifth percentile at $48,000.

Because many illustrators freelance and work on different types of projects—including packaging, annual reports, textbooks, and storybooks—salary information is far from uniform. Salaries can range from $18,000 to $65,000 or more. Salaries for medical illustrators are higher but also vary widely based on experience and type of work. Graduates from accredited schools of medical illustration working for institutions can expect to start at $40,000 to $45,000 per year, according to the Association of Medical Illustrators. Experienced illustrators might earn $45,000 to $75,000 per year.

Cartoonists drawing for syndication have similarly flexible pay scales but the potential to do incredibly well if enough newspapers pick up their comic strips. Syndicates generally split revenues fifty-fifty with the artist.

Meet Some Commercial Artists

Corina Brown, Graphic Designer

"I have always enjoyed art, and it came easy to me," says Corina Brown, owner and president of Interplanetary Design of Los Angeles. "Then, after I started college, I knew I wanted to be in broadcast design and films." She received her degree in graphic design and advertising from Western Washington University and also trained in broadcast design. After working for the Fox affiliate in Seattle for several years, she started her own company.

"When you start your own company, there is work that would be required for any start-up business. For example, I work online looking for new business, making cold calls, and communicating with existing customers. I do print work from my house, but when I get a broadcast job, I travel to the station's location and work on opens, promos, and other exciting stuff.

"I am very happy with my career—I am able to make my job what I want out of it. I love being my own boss; it pays well while I'm working; and I love to travel. But what I like least of all is that it gets stressful trying to get work. Also, there are more bills when you own your own company.

"I would advise others to figure out what direction in graphic design they would like to go in and then take a chance. Just remember that you will have to work hard to get where you want to be."

Edward Pitkoff, Advertising Designer

"What attracted me to this field was the idea of doing great creative advertising that could convince a consumer to purchase a product," Edward Pitkoff, of Omaha, Nebraska, says. "Having a mentor early on in my career taught me how to marry the communication to the consumer so they could visualize themselves as part of the product."

Pitkoff attended the Philadelphia Museum School of Art, the Pennsylvania Academy of Fine Arts, Temple University, and the Studio School of Art and Design—all in Philadelphia. He earned a bachelor of arts degree and attended marketing and advertising seminars and television production and direction seminars at the School of Visual Arts in New York. After twelve years working as a designer, assistant art director, art director, and creative director, he formed Ed Pitkoff Studios. "Ed Pitkoff Studios then expanded and evolved into Creative Decisions, Inc., and there the story truly started," says Pitkoff, who served as company president.

"Don't ever be distracted," Pitkoff emphasizes. "Focus on the business of advertising. Always remember what's important—not what do I want to say to sell this product or service, but what would be compelling to the consumer and what do they want to hear, what do they want to buy. They, the consumers, are the judge of how well your message has come across. If the product sells, then you know your focused communication has reached its intended audience."

Karen L. Sullivan, Designer

"I began my career working in public relations for a college," Karen Sullivan says. "I was hired because of my ability to write news releases for the campus activities. Additional responsibilities were added once they realized I had the ability to design. That experience took me to printers and publishers. I began asking questions and started designing brochures for the college.

"I have always been critical of display advertising in newspapers and magazines. When there is too much copy, or the eye cannot follow the layout, I notice it. When I was working in public relations for the college, I asked the artists questions about why the design couldn't be changed. I started to read about graphics, but actually had a natural ability.

"My career changed during my next job in the capacity of manager of a printer in southern Delaware—Blue Hen Publishing. We published a weekly advertising tabloid as well as various printing jobs. At the time we had a Compugraphic typesetter. I did all the design and hand placed copy. Once I got into the business, I realized how much I liked working with shapes and color. I still enjoy the work. It continues to be different and always offers a challenge.

"The positions I held always included other responsibilities. At Blue Hen, I worked with the owner to promote the business. From that I learned marketing tools. Each time I was faced with another business task, I asked questions from people in the field and read about the subject. I consider promotion, marketing, design, advertising, and graphics to be part of a complete package to inform the public of services rendered.

"I consider myself to be very fortunate right now because I work out of my home. When I worked for a business, I would work as many as fifty or sixty hours a week. The atmosphere was tense. Deadlines, broken equipment, and impossible customers made it a stressful job. Now, I work when I have the business. I don't accept work from people I don't really want to work with. Well, that isn't entirely true. Sometimes I take work because the money is good, the work is easy, and I resolve to handle the client for a short period of time.

"What I like the most is the sense of accomplishment I derive from the work I do. I love to learn about various businesses and then take that knowledge into my design ideas. Being creative is a very exhilarating experience. I love working with words and presenting them to the world in an artistic and easy-to-understand format. The best thing is the reaction from people when they see the work. Most of the time they are in love with it and cannot believe how much it reflects what they do. Sometimes they want little changes and are afraid I will be upset. But I don't have a problem with that.

"The things I like the least are the inconsistencies of the business. The market is competitive. People want everything for nothing. That frustrates me. When I told a friend my rates, she was shocked and said, 'Oh, well, I wouldn't pay that.' I said, 'Well, then you will shop around and see that most agencies charge four times that much. Then you will call me.' I never apologize for my fees.

"I would advise others who are considering getting into this field to know what is happening in the market. It is important to understand the demographics in an area in order to understand how and where to market a product and the slant to take on a campaign or brochure. Keep records, write proposals out, get signatures from clients at each stage of approval. Here are some other tips:

1. I always have clients sign the proposal with the rates and ask for one-third up front (stipulated in the proposal letter).
2. When we come to the final proof stage, I get them to take the proof (with the word PROOF superimposed across the

pages—sorry, but I don't leave much room for trust) and review it well. When they sign off on it, any errors will be repaired at their expense (also stipulated in the contract or proposal letter), and they pay me another one-third.

3. Then I get the project printed. Working with printers takes another phase of negotiation. When the work is done, I collect the last one-third. Sometimes this is cut into halves. I leave them with the finished originals, and they work out printing or copying the information. I keep all my work stored on disk, which I hold for the customer.

"This plan has worked well for me, and it just might work as well for you!"

Laura Lee Lineberry, Art Director

"I joined the University of Alabama's design team in the fall of 1987 as a mechanical artist," Laura Lee Lineberry says. "My initial goal was to find a job that would also allow me to further my education—and what better place than at a major university? I was promoted to art director after a little over three years and have served in that capacity ever since."

Lineberry received her bachelor of arts degree in visual communications from Florida State University in Tallahassee in 1984. She did some postgraduate work at Troy State University in Troy, Alabama, and received a master of arts in advertising and public relations from the University of Alabama in Tuscaloosa.

"So few people these days are lucky enough to be in a profession that allows them to do what they love to do best," Lineberry says. "I love solving design problems. Each new job is a challenge, much like a puzzle where my job is to find the best way to put all the pieces together. I love the fact that it never gets monotonous. Every job is a new challenge.

"I once worked for a small offset printing company in Fort Lauderdale that specialized in weekly newspaper magazines and shoppers. It was literally a sweatshop where our employer would work us forty hours in two and a half days, then send us home for the rest of the week in order to avoid paying us overtime. We sometimes would work from 7 A.M. until 2 A.M. the next morning! We couldn't go home until the job was done, and it had to be good work. We weren't just artists; we did everything (opaquing, stripping, burning plates)! At the time, I absolutely hated it. But it introduced me to all the different aspects of print production. It not only made me a much faster worker, it also made me more knowledgeable when talking with vendors and clients. Plus, I could actually say I was a stripper in Fort Lauderdale with an ounce of pride!

"I'm rather fortunate that most workdays now really are eight-hour days. Occasionally, there's a need to stay until the deadline is met, but I work with a strong team of writers and designers. We all wish we had more time, but the jobs meet all deadlines, and our clients are happy. We are generally working on more than eighty active jobs at any given time. I can't say that it's a real relaxed environment—we stay extremely busy and often complain that we need extra staff.

"I oversee all the design jobs that pass through our office. I have full design responsibility—if a designer goofs, I take the heat. We have a pretty strict proofing system and stick by it. The errors are few. Having worked for an agency, I learned that job security depended solely on the accounts held by that agency. I saw people come and go with each account gained or lost. Here at the university, the accounts are 98 percent on campus (departments, colleges, schools within the university). While the clients are not forced to use our services, most of them choose to, and security is never a source of concern. So, job security is a plus!

"On the downside, we are a small group with a huge workload. And unfortunately a twenty-minute design is never as good as a design given the proper amount of attention. We sometimes have to compromise our designs for the sake of time (or lack of time).

"In my early years, my goal was to be the best designer ever. I wanted people to look at my publications and see nothing more than the incredible design work I created. Once I matured, and my ego had deflated a bit, I learned that my job was not only to design but to lead the viewer into the publication, to read it. If the viewer couldn't get past the design, then I failed. A great design does not necessarily mean 'breaking new ground.' A great design is one that makes the piece work as a whole. Design for your audience, not just for yourself."

Faith Gowan, Art Director

Faith Gowan is the art director for Blue Mountain Arts, a publisher of greeting cards, books, calendars, and other products. She received her bachelor of fine arts degree in graphic design from the Philadelphia College of Art.

"Both of my parents were illustrators and designers, so I grew up surrounded by art," she says. "I've always liked to do design—via fabric, photography, paint, and so forth. And I wanted to pursue an area of art that would allow me to make a living. I didn't want to wait tables and do my art on the side. I think that because I'd watched my parents doing commercial art for years, it didn't have the stigma for me of being commercial and therefore not 'real' art. I guess also that I'd always liked to make things and had always wanted what I created to be useful in some way. Graphic design is all about communication and design.

"I did a lot of sewing and craft work as a teenager, and I still love to do that sort of thing. During a break in my college career, I managed a country and craft store for a while, doing crafts and teaching them as well as running the store. The craft work was fun but not really stimulating or challenging enough for me.

"When I first moved to Boulder after graduating from art school, I got a job working as a platemaker for a small printer, which was a very valuable experience for me. I learned about what happens to artwork after it leaves the designer's hands and what you need to provide to a printer to get a job printed successfully. It was similar to the experience of building a house to someone who wanted to become an architect.

"My job is more business and less creativity than I would ideally like, but that's probably the case with most jobs. The best days are spent doing creative design, working fairly independently and designing new products. Another very stimulating aspect of my job is the opportunity—and need—to learn new things and technologies all the time. When I studied graphic design, no one even thought that we'd eventually be using computers to do it. Learning this ever-changing technology, and learning how to get it to do what you want it to do, makes this career a real opportunity to grow. These days, I do some graphics for the Web, too, which has allowed me to add motion and animation to my design.

"A typical day involves some creative work but also keeping track of a lot of details of different deadlines, trying to meet various deadlines, managing people, and too much of just trying to get the job done. Our studio has a fairly relaxed and comfortable atmosphere, and there is a good camaraderie between employees. There are definitely new challenges every day.

"I most like the opportunity to be creative and to design pieces that I can be proud of. Also, I like the opportunity to keep learning. I least enjoy managing other employees.

"I would advise others to do what they love to do. Be creative. Try to get as much real-life experience as possible, even if that means doing design for little or no pay at first. Remember that computers are a great tool but not the *only* tool. Don't forget to draw, too!"

Ann P. O'Brien, Art Director, and Wendy Rubin, Creative Director

Ann P. O'Brien serves as art director and graphic designer, while Wendy Rubin is creative director and copywriter. Together, they are Rubin and O'Brien Ltd. of Glencoe, Illinois. O'Brien earned a bachelor of fine arts degree from Ohio Wesleyan and a master of arts degree from the University of Hawaii. Rubin earned a bachelor of education degree from the University of Illinois.

In 1983 Rubin was doing freelance copywriting. A friend was opening a store and needed an ad. Someone told Rubin to call O'Brien, and the rest is history.

"We find it extremely fulfilling to be able to work in a field that utilizes our talents," Rubin says. "We are creative thinkers. But what works for our clients is not just creativity but the ability we have to get the 'big idea'—to see beyond what is clever to what delivers results. That means that we understand the consumer. We have good instincts and marketing expertise."

"Even though advertising sounds like a 'glamour' job, it's really a lot of hard work," O'Brien says. "In running your own small business, you wear a lot of hats. There are production schedules, traffic schedules, proposals to write, new business to get, clients to deal with, and, of course, billing. And, in between, you create copy and design that press the right emotional buttons and move people to action. We work five days a week. Our day begins around 9 A.M. and ends about 5 or 6 P.M. It's a busy but relaxed atmosphere. We have an office manager in-house to assist. We develop marketing strategies and provide concept, copy, and design for brochures, annual reports, newsletters, ads, billboards, direct mail, and corporate identities, as well as write radio and television commercials."

"We like brainstorming for ideas and using the positive results of our labor," Rubin says. "We dislike the nitty-gritty details—all the proofing that needs to take place and the clients who argue about their bills."

"It's a wonderfully rewarding field," O'Brien says. "If you get that 'tingle' when ideas start to flow, and you're ready to rework an idea over and over until everyone is happy, then advertising is a great career. It is always challenging. You learn something new every day. If you are opening your own shop, be sure to have some business sense and get everything in writing. Ask clients for a deposit on any major expenses such as printing. Send out your bills on time. And always push yourself to the limits for good, workable, creative ideas."

Professional Associations

For information on careers in graphic design, contact:

American Institute of Graphic Arts
164 Fifth Avenue
New York, NY 10010
www.aiga.org

For information on art careers in publishing, contact:

Society of Publication Designers
475 Park Avenue South
New York, NY 10016
www.spd.org

Students in high school or college who are interested in careers as illustrators should contact:

Society of Illustrators
128 East Sixty-third Street
New York, NY 10021
www.societyillustrators.org

National Association of Schools of Art and Design
11250 Roger Bacon Drive, Suite 21
Reston, VA 20190
http://nasad.arts-accredit.org

For information on careers in medical illustration, contact:

Association of Medical Illustrators
6660 Del Monico Drive, Suite D-107
Colorado Springs, CO 80919
http://medical-illustrators.org

For information on careers in scientific illustration, contact:

Guild of Natural Science Illustrators
PO Box 652
Ben Franklin Station
Washington, DC 20044
www.gnsi.org

Color Marketing Group (CMG) is an international not-for-profit association of fifteen hundred color designers who forecast color directions one to three or more years in advance for all industries, manufactured products, and services. CMG offers international conferences, regional meetings, and workshops. For more information, contact:

Color Marketing Group
5845 Richmond Highway, #410
Alexandria, VA 22303
www.colormarketing.org

CHAPTER FIVE

Art Museum Professionals

*Museums and galleries are for people. Children need to grow up
in them. Art can give you excitement and energy. A painting
can do something for your spirit that nothing else can.*

—Riva Yares

A rt museums are buildings where objects of aesthetic value are preserved and displayed. Art museums have a variety of functions, including acquiring, conserving, and exhibiting works of art; providing art education for the general public; and conducting art history research.

Art museums can be classified into two major categories: private museums, under the authority of a board of trustees composed of private citizens and a director hired by the board; and public museums, administered directly by the national or local government.

In addition, art museums fall into two basic types: the general museum, presenting a broad range of works from early times to the present; and museums that specialize in one particular era, artist, region, or type of art.

In the past, art museums functioned mainly as storehouses for objects, but in recent years their role has been greatly expanded. More and more large art museums try to serve the interests of the community in which they are located. In addition to exhibiting their own collections, many museums develop special traveling exhibitions that are lent to other institutions for display. They also conduct guided tours of their collections, publish catalogs and books, provide lectures and other educational programs to members of the general public, and offer art classes to students.

A Look at Art Museum Careers

With all these varied roles, art museums now offer a wealth of employment opportunities to job seekers. Here are some job titles that hold special appeal for color connoisseurs.

Art Curator

Curators in art museums are responsible for the preservation of the collection and for implementing its visual accessibility to the public. The curator is usually an art historian, knowledgeable about the physical properties of handmade objects. While curators have a general background in the history of art, they usually specialize in a given area.

Large museums with diversified collections employ several curators for the different departments, such as American, European, modern, Asian, primitive, decorative arts, and photography.

Curators oversee the collections and participate in obtaining new acquisitions. They also verify the authenticity of paintings or objects by researching the provenance, documents attesting to previous owners and exhibitors.

Curators also supervise the installation of the museum's permanent collection. They determine the number of objects to be shown and decide when they'll be shown. Working with the exhibit designer, the curator also plans how objects or paintings will be displayed.

Assistant Curator. Depending on where they are employed, assistant curators could be responsible for studying and working on the permanent collection, organizing special exhibitions, conducting research, writing catalogs and art books, creating label and brochure copy for exhibitions, arranging for the display of different objects in the galleries, handling correspondence with the general public, answering inquiries, helping scholars with research, and administering loan requests to other museums.

Associate Curator/Curatorial Assistant. Associate curators and/or curatorial assistants report directly to the curator and help with the varied tasks the profession demands.

Moving Up the Curatorial Ladder. Of course, it's every assistant curator's hope to one day become a curator. Usually more money and prestige are involved with a promotion. However, to move ahead, a curator has to be willing to change locations. But opportunities can be limited, and sometimes it's better to stay right where you are. You need to balance the benefits of a move with potential drawbacks. Moving to a museum with a weaker collection than the one you are currently working with for a better job title, for example, might not pay off.

On the other hand, if you're interested in getting onto a director track, going to a smaller museum might be a good career move. You could be a director at a small museum, then eventually a director at a bigger museum. Keep in mind, however, that the more administrative your job becomes, the less work you can do as a scholar.

Exhibit Designer

Exhibit designers focus on three things: the number of images or objects in an exhibit, the information they want to convey to the public, and the amount of square footage available for display.

These art museum professionals convert images into videodiscs, storyboards, or a series of slide presentations. They make scale models and put bids out for construction contractors. In some cases they write the script and labels for the exhibit and conduct audience research to see how the public reacts to the exhibit.

Some museums follow the traditional model, in which the curator passes abstract ideas over to the designer, who then translates them into a physical presentation. The curator is responsible for content and ideas and the written word, while the designer is responsible for the environment and the aesthetics and graphic design. In a more modern approach—a collaborative exhibition development—a team of professionals works together.

Many small and even midsize institutions do not have room in their budgets for a specialist exhibit designer. In a situation such as that, one or two people, the director or the curator, might perform the functions of an exhibit designer in addition to the duties of their own specialty. Or, in some cases, the museum will contract with an outside firm for exhibit design work. Some large institutions, such as the Smithsonian Institution, for example, employ more than twenty exhibit designers and assistants.

Art and Object Conservator

Many people think that once something valuable gets into a museum it's safe, but, unfortunately, it can decay on the museum's walls or shelves just as it would decay on yours at home. Many different conditions contribute to that decaying process: light, variations in humidity and temperature, pollutants, pests, and accidental damage. Conservators concern themselves with preventing and repairing that decay.

They apply solvents and cleaning agents to damaged and faded paintings to clean the surfaces. They reconstruct or retouch damaged areas and apply preservatives to protect the paintings.

Being a conservator is a team effort. Often the conservator and curator both look under the microscope and discuss what they should do with a piece that's damaged, whether to leave it alone or just stabilize it to avoid further degradation.

Conservators also deal with the exhibits department, providing information on how to build a mount for an object so that the object is supported, for example. They provide much of the information that is displayed on labels and arrange for proper lighting levels so the colors don't fade.

Conservators also work closely with exhibit designers, curators, collection managers, and registrars when they're planning a new show or transporting art objects. How an object is supported or wrapped so it can go to another museum without damage often falls into the conservator's realm.

And though working with visiting scholars is usually part of a collection manager's job, conservators often instruct students about the correct way to handle art objects.

Registrar

Registrars in art museums keep track of the location of all the various works of art in the museum's collection. Paintings and other art objects are often moved to different areas within a museum or transported to other museums for exhibition. Because of this, it is necessary to maintain accurate files.

Registrars are also responsible for shipping objects and obtaining insurance. They take care of the packing, make the transportation arrangements, arrange for couriers, and keep an archive of all of the works that are loaned to the museum.

In some smaller museums, the registrars will sometimes check the condition of objects and perform other exhibition duties. At larger museums, where the separate curatorial departments have their own storage rooms and control their own inventory, registrars will sometimes do spot checking on a yearly basis to make sure their records are correct.

Registrars often work closely with the curatorial staff. Basically, a curator decides what to have in a particular show and gives the registrar the list of all the objects. Then the registrar has to make sure the loan agreements are signed and in place, make all the packing arrangements, contact the borrowers or the lenders to the museum, coordinate scheduling of shipments and courier arrangements, and then make arrangements for the unpacking of those objects. The registrar also coordinates with the conservation staff to check the condition of the works.

Collections Manager

The collections manager supervises, numbers, catalogs, and stores the specimens within each division of the museum. The collections manager provides support for the curator, exhibit designer, conservator, and registrar.

Photographer

Many art museums keep a professional photographer on staff to provide photographic documentation of the various fine arts collections. Photographers also find work in planetariums and other types of museums. Photographers must oversee the photography of general museum events and activities, be responsible for studio and darkroom facilities, and manage personnel issues for any assistants.

Educator

Almost all museums provide some sort of educational programming for the public. Educators and program developers design and arrange these programs. They explain the exhibits, conduct classes, workshops, lectures, and tours, and often offer outreach programs to the schools or local community.

Training and Qualifications

Since museums offer so many diverse careers, the avenues of training leading to these professions are equally diverse. An art conservator would have a background different from a curator's; an educator's preparation would differ from an exhibit designer's.

In addition, different museums often look for different qualifications. Some prefer candidates to have an advanced degree or certificate in museology or museum studies. Others expect to hire professionals with strong academic concentrations in, for example, art history. Most are impressed with a combination of academic and hands-on training earned through internships or volunteer programs.

There are, however, several skills and personal traits common to all museum professionals. First, all museum workers need to have excellent interpersonal skills. Educators and exhibit designers present information to staff and visitors; curators supervise staff and cultivate contacts with donors and other community members. The ability to get along with others and to work well as a team is a vital asset in museum work.

Of equal importance is the ability to communicate through the written word. Museums meet their missions with their collections of objects, but to do so, museum workers must have strong writing skills, which show themselves in grant applications, exhibition catalogs, brochures, administrative and scholarly reports, training and educational materials, legal agreements, interpretive labeling for exhibits, object records, and much more.

Computer skills are also important. More and more museums are relying on computers to keep track of their collections, to design labels, and to produce catalogs and brochures, as well as other functions. Facility with a variety of software programs can only be an asset to a prospective museum worker.

Traditionally, new employees in the field of museum work have completed bachelor's and master's degrees in academic disciplines appropriate to the intended careers. Curators for art museums have studied art and art history; curators for natural history museums have studied biology, anthropology, archeology, and so on. And while such a background still serves as the main foundation for successful museum work, over the last several decades, more and more people have explored university programs offering practical and theoretical training in the area of museum studies. Courses such as museum management, curatorship, fundraising, exhibition development, and law and museums offer a more specific approach to the work at hand. This, coupled with a broad background in liberal arts or specialization in an academic discipline, provides the museum professional with a knowledge base better designed to serve the needs of the museum.

Whatever your course of study, currently most museums require an upper-level degree, either in an academic discipline or in museum studies, museum science, or museology. Also required is an intensive internship or record of long-term volunteer work. The internship is considered the most crucial practical learning experience and is generally a requirement in all programs. It can run from ten weeks to a year with varying time commitments per week.

Training for Curators

Employment as a curator generally requires graduate education and substantial practical or work experience. Many curators work in museums while completing their formal education in order to gain the hands-on experience that many employers seek when hiring.

In most museums, a master's degree in an appropriate discipline of the museum's specialty—for example, art, art history, or museum studies—is required for employment as a curator. Many employers prefer a doctoral degree. In small museums, curatorial positions may be available to individuals with a bachelor's degree. For some positions, an internship of full-time museum work supplemented by courses in museum practices is needed.

Training for Exhibit Designers

To become an exhibit designer, a degree or certification in graphic or industrial design, commercial art or communications arts, architecture, interior design, or studio arts can open the door for you. Exhibit designers should also have experience in exhibition design and related construction work with wood, metal, or plastics, usually obtained through graphic arts programs, museum studies programs, or internships. A portfolio of past and current work is necessary.

Desirable qualities for exhibit managers include the ability to conceptualize exhibit designs, skill in mechanical drawing, the ability to make refined aesthetic judgments, and supervisory experience to oversee the installation of exhibits.

Training for Conservators

Conservators are a group of highly trained professionals who have gone through a number of steps to gain their expertise. Training programs are few and, as a result, are very competitive.

According to the American Institute for Conservation of Historic and Artistic Works, a conservator must have:

- Appreciation for cultural property of all kinds and knowledge of their historic and sociological significance, their aesthetic qualities, and the technology of their production
- Aptitude for scientific and technical subjects
- Patience for meticulous and tedious work
- Good manual dexterity and color vision
- Intelligence and sensitivity for making sound judgments
- Ability to communicate effectively

During the course of a training program, student conservators are exposed to work with a variety of materials before going on to specialize in a particular area. They learn skills to prevent the deterioration of paintings, paper and books, fiber, textiles, ceramics, wood, furniture, and other objects. There are even conservators in architectural conservation and library and archives conservation.

Traditionally, training is gained through a graduate academic program, which takes from two to four years. Apprenticeships or internships are a vital part of training and are usually undertaken during the final year of study. Some programs might offer internships that run concurrently with classes.

Admission requirements for the various graduate programs differ, but prerequisites for all programs include courses in chemistry, art history, studio art, anthropology, and archaeology.

Some programs prefer candidates to already have a strong background in conservation, which can be gained through undergraduate apprenticeships and fieldwork in private, regional, or institutional conservation laboratories.

The names and addresses of the fourteen conservation degree and internship training programs currently active in North America are listed at the end of this chapter. Contact those that interest you for their specific admission requirements.

Training for Collections Managers

An undergraduate degree in the area of the museum's specialization is the minimum requirement for collections managers. An advanced degree in museum studies with a concentration in a specific discipline is recommended.

A collections manager must have knowledge of information management techniques and the ability to accurately identify objects within the museum's collection. Knowledge of security practices and environmental controls is also important.

Training for Photographers

Many photographers are self-taught; others receive their training in a variety of ways—through traditional art schools, university art and photography departments, and apprenticeships. A portfolio documenting your professional experience would be a requirement for employment.

Training for Educators

Educators usually possess a teaching certificate or have had teaching experience before they join a museum staff. A bachelor's degree and sometimes a master's degree in education or art history may be required.

Salaries

The Association of Art Museum Directors conducts an annual salary survey of both current and former AAMD members. The following figures are approximate averages of the responses received for 2003.

Chief curators	$72,000
Senior curators	$61,836
Curators of exhibitions	$52,000
Associate curators	$44,150
Assistant curators	$38,300
Curatorial assistants	$28,080
Photographers	$45,000
Directors of education	$53,800
Associate educators	$38,100
Assistant educators	$32,113
Educational assistants	$26,390
Registrars	$44,590
Associate registrars	$37,400
Assistant registrars	$30,000
Chief conservators	$72,807
Senior conservators	$60,800
Associate conservators	$44,909
Exhibition designers	$50,002

To receive the latest annual survey, contact either the Association of Art Museum Directors or the American Association of Museums. Both organizations are listed at the end of this chapter.

Strategies for the Job Hunt

Although formal academic training is vital to your resume, hands-on experience is of equal importance. Not only does hands-on experience provide a host of significant skills, it also allows the career explorer to make an informed decision about the suitability of museum work. Starting with a term of volunteer work, even before beginning a college program, will provide a better idea of what career options museums have to offer and whether these options are right for you.

Many museums rely heavily on volunteer energy and can place volunteers in almost every museum department, from tour guide and gift shop sales to assisting curators and exhibit designers. The easiest way to volunteer your time is to call a museum and ask to speak to the volunteer coordinator, who will work with you to match your interests with the museum's needs. Volunteer programs are usually flexible about the number of hours and days per week they expect from their volunteers.

Most academic museum studies programs require an internship before a degree or certificate can be awarded. In addition, many museums have their own internship programs that are offered to full-time students as well as recent graduates. You can check with your university department first to see what arrangements are traditionally made.

If the burden is on you to arrange an internship, either during your academic program or after you've graduated, contact the museum's internship coordinator. If the museum has no formal internship program, talk first to a museum staff member to determine where there might be a need. Then, you can write a proposal incorporating your interests in a department where help will be appreciated.

Internships can be either paid or unpaid and are usually a more formal arrangement than volunteering. The number of hours and weeks are structured, and the intern might be expected to complete a specific project during his or her time there. Often, college credit can be earned.

The American Association of Museums (AAM) has published a resource report called "Standards and Guidelines for Museum

Internships." It covers what museums expect from their interns and what interns can and should expect from the museum. It is available through the AAM's bookstore, whose information is listed at the end of this chapter. Later, when it comes time to look for a job, a successful internship or stint of volunteer work can open the door at the training institution or at other museums.

Meet a Museum Professional

Ronnie Lee Roese, Executive Director

"I've worked in museums all my life," says Ronnie Lee Roese, executive director of the Biblical Arts Center in Dallas, Texas. "I started when I was in high school and continued to work my way through college by working at a museum. Upon graduation I was offered a full-time job as an exhibit designer at the museum where I was working during college."

Roese earned a bachelor of science degree in architecture from the University of Texas at Arlington and also attended numerous career development seminars over the years, including two programs with the Graduate School of Design at Harvard, the Smithsonian, and other programs with the American Association of Museums (AAM), the Texas Association of Museums (TAM), and the American Association for State and Local History (AASLH).

"I find that working in museums allows a lot of personal freedom," Roese says. "Working conditions tend to be very easygoing. I'm a very independent person, a freethinker, and need the space to do my own thing!

"The gentleman who hired me for my first museum job moved to Dallas from the small town in central Texas where we were living. He told me to look him up if I ever came to his new town, so I did, and he hired me to work part-time as I went to college. After college he hired me full-time. Under his directorship, I went from being a curatorial assistant to assistant curator to curator of exhibits to director of museum services. After working in that capacity for a while, I decided there was no room for advancement and took a director position in a small town. I disliked the small-town politics, so I returned and was immediately offered my old job of director of museum services. I worked there for a number of years before I was offered the job I now have.

"The board of my current organization was given my name by the former director, and they contacted me, interviewed me, and hired me within a week's time. I told the board that I would antic-ipate staying on for only a year or so, and it's been over ten years. That's because I love my job. As director, I am responsible for everything. I have assembled a very reliable staff that handles almost everything, except major decisions. My work week is flex-ible, although I generally work Monday through Friday from 8:30 A.M. to 5 P.M. There is also evening work involved with recep-tions, meetings, and such. I try to stay very involved with the day-to-day operations of the center because I want to stay in touch with it.

"What I like most about my job is the fact that it allows me to be the independent person that I am. Because I have such a reli-able staff, I can travel as much as I like. (I remain in constant com-munication, though.) I'm in a very unique position in that we have very little board input into the operation of the center. The board has given me complete control!

"The major downside of my job is the fact that I will never make as much money as friends or family who work in the for-profit industry. There is also no room for advancement where I am now, unless I want to make a major change, such as move to a new city or state.

"My number one piece of advice for someone interested in a career in the museum field is to volunteer in a museum! Get your foot in the door by volunteering; get experience by volunteering; and most of all, get firsthand information about whether or not this is the profession for you by volunteering. Opportunities abound for volunteers; it doesn't have to be more than a couple of hours a month on a weekend or maybe after school. Offer to do menial jobs and other chores no one else wants to do just to get the exposure. It can mean the beginning of the most perfect career!"

Professional Associations

The following list of associations can be used as a valuable resource guide in locating additional information about specific careers. Many of the organizations publish newsletters listing job and internship opportunities, and still others offer an employment service to members. A quick look at the organizations' names will give you an idea of the scope of museum programs.

National and International Associations

American Association for Museum Volunteers
4050 North Tocasierra Trail
Flagstaff, AZ 86001
www.acnatsci.org/hosted/aamv

American Association of Museums
1575 Eye Street NW, Suite 400
Washington, DC 20005
www.aam-us.org

American Institute for Conservation of Historic and
  Artistic Works
1717 K Street NW, Suite 200
Washington, DC 20006
http://aic.standford.edu

Archives of American Art
Reference Services
Smithsonian Institution
PO Box 37012
Victor Building, Room 2200, MRC 937
Washington, DC 20013
http://artarchives.si.edu

Association for Volunteer Administration
2500 Grenoble Road
Richmond, VA 23294
www.avaintl.org

Association of Art Museum Directors
41 East Sixty-fifth Street
New York, NY 10021
www.aamd.org

Association of Children's Museums
1300 L Street NW, Suite 975
Washington, DC 20005
www.childrensmuseums.org

Association of College and University Museums and Galleries
Philip and Muriel Berman Museum of Art
Ursinus College
601 East Main Street
Collegeville, PA 19426
www.acumg.org

Canadian Museums Association
280 Metcalfe Street, Suite 400
Ottawa, ON K2P 1R7
Canada
www.museums.ca

Independent Curators International
799 Broadway, Suite 205
New York, NY 10003
www.ici-exhibitions.org

International Association of Museum Facilities Administrators
c/o High Museum of Art
1280 Peachtree Road NE
Atlanta, GA 30309
www.iamfa.org

International Institute for Conservation of Historic and
    Artistic Works
6 Buckingham Street
London WC2N 6BA
England
www.iiconservation.org

International Museum Theatre Alliance
c/o Wildlife Theatre
Central Park Zoo
New York, NY 10021
www.imtal.org

Museum Computer Network
232–329 March Road
Box 11
Ottawa, ON K2K 2E1
Canada
www.mcn.edu

Museum Education Roundtable
621 Pennsylvania Avenue SE
Washington, DC 20003
www.mer-online.org

Museum Reference Center
Smithsonian Institution
Arts and Industries Building, Room 2235
900 Jefferson Drive SW
Washington, DC 20560
www.sil.si.edu/BranchBrochures/mrc-bro.htm

National African-American Museum and Cultural Complex
PO Box 30170
Washington, DC 20030
www.aamuseum.org

Smithsonian Center for Education and Museum Studies
Smithsonian Institution
Arts & Industries Building, Room 2235
900 Jefferson Drive SW
Washington, DC 20560
http://museumstudies.si.edu

Regional Museum Associations

Association of Midwest Museums
PO Box 11940
St. Louis, MO 63112
www.midwestmuseums.org

Mid-Atlantic Association of Museums
The Carroll Mansion
800 East Lombard Street
Baltimore, MD 21202
www.midatlanticmuseums.org

Mountain-Plains Museums Association
7110 West David Drive
Littleton, CO 80128
www.mountplainsmuseums.org

New England Museum Association
22 Mill Street, Suite 409
Arlington, MA 02476
www.nemanet.org

Southeastern Museums Conference
PO Box 9003
Atlanta, GA 31106
www.semcdirect.net

Western Museums Conference
PO Box 13314
Oakland, CA 94661
www.westmuse.org

Conservation Degree and Internship Training Programs

The following symbols, in parentheses below, designate the level of training the following conservation training programs offer: U–Undergraduate; G–Graduate; P–Postgraduate; I–Internships; C–Courses.

Art Conservation Department (G)
Buffalo State College
230 Rockwell Hall
1300 Elmwood Avenue
Buffalo, NY 14222
www.buffalostate.edu/depts/artconservation

Art Conservation Department (UGP)
University of Delaware
303 Old College
Newark, DE 19716
www.udel.edu/artcons

Campbell Center for Historic Preservation Studies (C)
203 East Seminary
Mt. Carroll, IL 61053
www.campbellcenter.org

Canadian Conservation Institute (GPI)
Training and Information Division
1030 Innes Road
Ottawa, ON K1A 0M5
Canada
www.cci-icc.gc.ca

Graduate School of Architecture, Planning, and
   Preservation (G)
Columbia University
1172 Amsterdam Avenue
New York, NY 10027
www.arch.columbia.edu

Conservation Center of the Institute of Fine Arts (GC)
New York University
The Stephen Chan House
14 East Seventy-eighth Street
New York, NY 10021
www.nyu.edu/gsas/dept/fineart/ifa

Getty Conservation Institute (C)
1200 Getty Center Drive, Suite 700
Los Angeles, CA 90049
www.getty.edu/conservation/institute

Johns Hopkins University (P)
Department of Materials Science and Engineering
102 Maryland Hall
3400 North Charles Street
Baltimore, MD 21218
www.jhu.edu/~matsci/index.html
(Ph.D. in materials science with a concentration in conservation
science, sponsored by the Smithsonian Center for Materials Research
and Education)

Master of Art Conservation Program (G)
Department of Art, Ontario Hall
Queens University
Kingston, ON K7L 3N6
Canada
http://qsilver.queensu.ca/arth/programs_artc.html

Smithsonian Center for Materials Research and
    Education (IC)
Museum Support Center
4210 Silver Hill Road
Suitland, MD 20746
www.si.edu/scmre

Straus Center for Conservation (PI)
Harvard University Art Museums
32 Quincy Street
Cambridge, MA 02138
www.artmuseums.harvard.edu/straus/index.html

University of Denver (C)
School of Art and Art History
2121 East Asbury Avenue
Denver, CO 80208
www.du.edu/art
   *(Preconservation aide program and certificate in preconservation
   studies)*

University of Pennsylvania (G)
Graduate Program in Historic Preservation
115 Meyerson Hall
Philadelphia, PA 19104
www.design.upenn.edu/new/hist

University of Texas at Austin (G)
School of Information
Preservation and Conservation Education Programs for
   Libraries and Archives
One University Station, D7000
Austin, TX 78712
www.gslis.utexas.edu/programs

Art Gallery Professionals

A picture is a poem without words.
—Horace

Art galleries—a perfect place for color connoisseurs—come in all shapes and sizes and are usually privately owned. Some are small, operating with only one or two employees in addition to the director/owner. Large galleries, especially those in New York City, maintain a staff of ten, fifteen, twenty, or more people, most of whom carry the title of assistant director.

Art galleries showcase the work of several artists or feature just one at a time. They sometimes also focus on a specific historical period, category of art, or geographical region. In this vein, they are similar to specialized museums that focus on the works of a single artist or a specific period or category.

However, that is where the similarities end. Art galleries operate very differently from art museums. While a museum depends on membership and grants for its support, an art gallery must earn its owner and employees their living through the sale of artworks to the public.

Profile of Art Gallery Workers

Most gallery owners are art lovers, and knowledgeable ones at that. You can't open and operate a gallery without having a strong love as well as a deep understanding of the world of art. The same is true for other art gallery employees. Anyone involved with the selling and display of art must be a true fan. In fact, you'll often find studio artists working in art galleries as a way to earn extra money to make ends meet. And where better to do that than in a setting that allows constant contact with other artists and art lovers?

But being an art lover isn't the only quality art gallery workers possess. A flair for selling and the ability to discuss works of art are also necessary. A demeanor that is persuasive and extroverted but not pushy and an ability to instill confidence are important. Clients rely on the choices and advice of art gallery professionals when making investments in art.

Art gallery owners must also have a sense of how best to display the artwork. They must know how to place paintings in relation to one another and make sure there are no conflicts in image. For example, puting an ethereal kind of painting next to a visceral abstract could destroy the the viewer's appreciation for the sensitive painting.

A Look at Art Gallery Careers

The following are typical job titles found in art galleries.

Director/Owner

The owner of an art gallery is responsible for every aspect of running the gallery, from selecting the artists to designing the layout of the show, hanging the artwork, promoting the show and the gallery, and selling to clients.

Assistant Director

A large gallery could have ten or more assistant directors. They work directly with the owner, representing the gallery and reflecting the owner's taste. Assistant directors work with customers, or clients, as they are frequently called, discussing the artwork and making sales.

Packager/Maintenance Worker

Most large galleries have "backroom staff," personnel responsible for packaging purchased pieces of art for shipping. Maintenance workers, under the direction of the director or an assistant director, hang the paintings in designated positions.

In many cases, artists take jobs as packagers or maintenance personnel in galleries to support themselves while they paint and work at establishing themselves in their own careers. The contacts they make allow them to maintain involvement in the art world—at least at some level.

It's also a good way for someone aiming for an assistant director position to get a foot in the door. It puts you in contact with the art arena, allowing you an opportunity to learn. You'll hear why they're "showing" someone and how they're exhibiting the work and what is being done to publicize the show. It's always worthwhile to know every aspect of the business, and these so-called menial jobs are very important.

Framer

Most small galleries farm out their work to frame shops, but the larger galleries often have a framer on staff who is skilled in cutting mats for prints and making frames for canvases. However, most artists deliver their work to galleries already framed, so the need for professional framers hired directly by a gallery is small.

Receptionist

Many large galleries, especially those in New York, hire receptionists to greet customers and answer questions over the phone. They must be knowledgeable about the artwork shown and be able to intelligently discuss different aspects of the work. Most receptionists have a degree in art; many use the position as a stepping-stone to assistant director.

Starting an Art Gallery

Art gallery owners acquire art in a couple of ways. Once established, art gallery owners have little to do, other than wait for talented artists to seek them out. And the owner of a gallery with a well-respected name doesn't have to wait too long. Once you have a track record, you reach a plateau where the artist knows your reputation and wants to be in your stable of artists. Being showcased by a name gallery has launched many an art career.

But when you're just starting out, you have to trust your taste and look for talent that has not yet been discovered. Gallery owners often travel throughout the United States and Europe in search of talent.

Gallery owners spend a lot of time, either at home or abroad, talking to artists and viewing slides. The artist might be wonderful, with beautiful art, but then you also have to evaluate whether you'll be able to sell that art. Each space on the wall costs you a certain amount of money. You have to be able to meet your expenses and make every inch of wall space pay for itself. Some new owners choose to specialize in a particular art form in order to establish themselves as experts in that area. They then look for artists working in that category. This helps also to attract clients who share the gallery owner's tastes. Seasoned gallery owners will tell you that they never sell a painting—they sell themselves first.

Strategies for the Job Hunt

Even if you're considering owning your own gallery, the best advice is to gain experience first, working for an existing gallery. But securing a job interview at the larger galleries isn't always an easy task. A good place to start is to ask for an informational interview (a chance to pick the owner's brain). While there might not be any openings, your interest will be noted, and if something should come up, you'd be on the list. This is also a great way to make contacts and start your networking. There might not be a job available at that particular gallery, but chances are the owner is in touch with other galleries as well.

Other people to contact for informational interviews are museum curators and directors. With each person you talk to, you're putting yourself in the loop.

Location, Location, Location

Where you choose to set up shop is truly crucial and should not be an area to skimp on costs. Look for a space in the best location, even though it might be more expensive. If you can be in a cultural area, near a museum, that would be ideal. A very inexpensive space off the beaten track is not the way to go.

Training and Qualifications

The background most assistant directors need is a knowledge of art on a historic level. If you are aware of the evolution of art and know what happened fifty or one hundred years ago, you will be able to speak the language, which makes your selling capability much greater.

To prepare for a job, a degree in art (either art history or applied arts) is beneficial, though you can obtain a position without it. You're also evaluated on your presence, how well you can describe the art, and how extroverted you are with clients. Sales skills can be learned, but you must have a sincerity about this kind of work.

Salaries

Most galleries work on a 50 percent fee basis with the artist, meaning the sale price is split evenly between the artist and the gallery. With a very popular artist, the gallery might take only 30 percent.

The cost of the artwork could range from $2,000 for a small wooden mask to $10,000 or even $50,000 or more for paintings. Popular artists are very attractive to gallery owners because of the added attention and larger following they bring to the gallery.

The expenses involved with owning a gallery are minimal, compared with other types of businesses. You don't pay for your stock until it is sold. Expenses up front include rent, some storage space, track lighting, and little else. Galleries require only a desk, a chair, and expanses of clean walls painted white. Regular expenses include advertising costs, brochures, catalogs, announcements, insurance, utilities, and employee salaries.

Professional Associations

Art Dealers Association of America, Inc.
575 Madison Avenue
New York, NY 10022
www.artdealers.org

Association of College and University Museums and Galleries
Philip and Muriel Berman Museum of Art
Ursinus College
601 East Main Street
Collegeville, PA 19426
www.acumg.org

CHAPTER SEVEN

Art Educators

The first hope of a painter who feels hopeful about painting is the hope that the painting will move, that it will live outside its frame.
—Gertrude Stein

For some, a teaching career in art or an art-related subject is a dream come true. These natural teachers best express their love of and skill in a subject area by sharing it and encouraging it in others. Although most art educators probably still practice their art, they do it more for self-expression and self-satisfaction than as a way to make a living.

For many others, though, a job as an art instructor is a means to an end. The teaching job takes a companion role to the main career as a studio or commercial artist. One of the reasons artists work as teachers is because the percentage of people who succeed in the arts is very small. Teaching is a logical choice for artists who want to use their talents on a daily basis. Teaching also provides the security of a regular paycheck and health benefits that a freelancing career might not offer—at least not when you are just starting out.

In addition, because of the generous vacation periods—two months in summer and a week or more at winter and spring breaks—most teachers enjoy, artists have ample time to pursue their own artwork. There are also many settings where art teachers can work part-time, leaving even more hours free for studio or commercial art undertakings.

Settings for Art Teachers

Because the qualifications and formal training needed vary depending on the job setting, it's important first to look at the options open to you. You might automatically think of teaching in public or private schools, but the range of employers for art instructors is much wider than for teachers in other subject areas.

Here is a sampling of some possible employers to investigate:

Adult education centers
Alternative schools
Art schools
Colleges and universities
Community colleges
Community or senior centers
Department of Defense dependent schools
Discovery centers
Group homes
Halfway houses
International schools
Museums
Parks departments
Prisons
Private schools
Public schools
Recreation centers
Rehabilitation centers
Religious organizations
Summer camps

Training and Qualifications

There are two schools of thought on the training and qualifications an art educator should have. Many artists feel that an artist is inherently able to teach art, that the ability to share technique and encourage proficiency is a natural extension of an artist's creativity. They believe that when a degree is necessary, it should be a degree in art, as opposed to art education. In other words, you must be able to do what you teach.

However, many hiring bodies, particularly schools, believe that art teachers should have the same credentials as teachers of any other subject. This viewpoint holds that the ability to create art doesn't necessarily guarantee the ability to teach.

But do all employers demand a degree of their art instructors? The answer to that is a definite "no." In many settings, your skill, as demonstrated by your portfolio or the name you have made for yourself, would be in high demand—with or without a degree. Accomplished artists are often invited as guest speakers to teach studio classes or workshops at various art schools or community centers. For example, a working potter who has a portfolio or sample pieces to show could be qualified on those credentials alone to teach in a private studio, at a summer camp, at a city park or recreation center, in a prison, in a group home, or in a variety of other settings.

Those who are just starting out can still find employment without a degree. But this employment is generally part-time, usually with an hourly wage. To pursue a teaching career full-time and to earn a professional-level salary, a bachelor's degree is the usual minimum requirement. To work in most public school systems, it is also necessary to have a state teaching certificate. Though not a common practice, some public school districts make provisions to grant temporary certification to noncredentialed teachers, usually because the districts have had difficulty securing teachers because of location or pay scale.

Some private and alternative schools will also hire noncertified teachers, but with the high supply and relatively small demand for art teachers, they, too, often require teachers to have the same credentials that public schools do.

In art schools and colleges, community colleges and four-year universities, bachelor's degrees are the minimum requirement and in most cases master's degrees or doctorates are necessary. While those teaching K–12 must have a teaching certificate and a degree in art education, those at the university level would most likely have degrees in fine art—usually a bachelor's of fine arts as well as a master's of fine arts.

Additional Qualities for Teachers

No matter what subject area is involved—whether it be art, science, or air-conditioning repair—there are qualities and skills that all teachers must possess. In addition to being knowledgeable in the subject, they must have the ability to communicate, inspire trust and confidence, and motivate students, as well as understand their educational and emotional needs.

Prospective art teachers should also be organized, dependable, and patient, as well as creative. Stamina, commitment, and a sense of humor are also important. These are qualities that no degree can document.

Working Conditions

Working conditions will vary, depending on the teaching assignment. Educators working in school systems generally work the same number of hours and teach the same number of classes as teachers of other subjects. They might also be responsible for monitoring lunch periods or coaching after-school sports.

They might have small classes with highly motivated students in an adult education program, or they might work in an alternative school with large numbers of troubled teens who have little or no interest in art but are required to take the classes.

In public school settings, students could come to class with an array of emotional and physical handicaps as well as behavior problems, which can subject teachers to high levels of stress. In addition to the students, teachers also have to deal with other teachers and administrators. In some settings it might seem as if paperwork is more important than art.

Supplies and equipment might be limited because of funding, or they might be state-of-the-art. Also, depending on the setting, evening and weekend work might be required. Working hours might be guaranteed, in a public school for example, or paychecks could be dependent upon the number of students who enroll in art classes.

Strategies for the Job Hunt

Art educators have a number of resources they can tap into to help with the job search.

The Internet

You can quickly survey the types of positions that are available around the country, likely pay, useful associations, and ideal employers, as well as gain crucial background information on an institution or organization before you appear for an interview.

Use the Web to build your base of knowledge about what type of position you want, what skills are necessary to get it, and what people you might need to talk to in the process. Start with industry websites (listed at the end of this chapter), then check out online classifieds and sites for individual schools, institutions, or organizations.

College Career Placement Centers

Most colleges maintain career centers that receive regular job listings. They are posted on bulletin boards or housed in ring binders. You can also leave your resume on file at many career centers. Prospective employers often contact college career offices looking for likely candidates.

Internships and Volunteering

Art educators, especially those hoping to land a museum job, will find internships and volunteering stints to be the most important keys in that particular setting. Museums cry out for volunteer help, and internships can be arranged through your university. Once in the door, make yourself indispensable. When a job opening occurs, you'll be there on the spot, ready to step in.

Direct Contact

Look through the phone book to find likely employers such as recreation centers or the local YMCA or similar organizations. Call for an appointment or walk in on a "cold call."

Set your portfolio or resume down on the appropriate desk, and you might find you have just landed yourself a job. This approach works best in adult education centers, community centers, and related settings.

The Chronicle of Higher Education

This is the old standby for those seeking positions within two- and four-year colleges and universities. It is a weekly publication available by subscription or in any library or college placement office.

Placement Agencies

For private schools particularly, both at home and abroad, placement agencies can provide a valuable source for finding jobs. Some charge both the employer and the prospective employee a fee. Others charge just one or the other.

Salaries

The size of your paycheck will be dependent upon the setting in which you work. Here is a look at the salary offerings of a few of the major employers of art educators.

School Systems

Median annual earnings for all teachers from kindergarten through secondary school ranged from $39,810 to $44,340 in 2002. These figures include both new teachers just starting out and those who have been on the job as long as twenty years or more. Your earnings will also vary depending upon the area of the country in which you work. Earnings in private schools are generally lower than they are in public schools.

In some schools, teachers earn extra pay for working with students in extracurricular activities. Many art teachers add to their income during the summer by producing and selling their own art or by working in related jobs.

Higher Education

Earnings vary according to faculty rank and type of institution and, in some cases, by field. Faculty in four-year institutions earn higher salaries, on the average, than those in two-year schools. In fact, those in two-year schools are often paid an hourly wage, which could range from $15 to $40 an hour.

According to figures from the National Center for Education Statistics and the Integrated Postsecondary Education Data System, salaries for full-time faculty on nine-month contracts averaged about $56,000 a year in 2002–2003. Those on eleven- or twelve-month contracts obviously earned more. Those starting as instructors could expect an average of $36,000 a year. Most college and university faculty enjoy some unique benefits, including access to campus facilities, tuition waivers for dependents, housing and travel allowances, and paid sabbatical leaves. Part-time faculty have fewer benefits than full-time faculty.

Adult Education

Earnings vary widely by subject, academic credentials, experience, and region of the country. Salaried adult education teachers who work full-time realize median earnings of approximately $34,000 a year. A new teacher might earn only in the low twenties. Part-timers are generally paid hourly wages and do not receive benefits or pay for preparation time outside of class.

Meet an Art Educator

Michele Lyons Lefkovitz, Art Teacher

"I became an artist when someone handed me a box of crayons when I was in kindergarten at the age of four," says Michele Lyons Lefkovitz, an elementary art teacher for Forest Glen Elementary School (an International Magnet Program) in Indianapolis, Indiana.

Lefkovitz attended the University of Cincinnati College of Design, Architecture, Art, and Planning (DAAP) and earned both bachelor and master of arts in education degrees from the Herron School of Art at Indiana University in Indianapolis. She is recognized as a Certified Arts and Crafts Teacher for the state of Indiana and has earned a Life License to teach kindergarten through twelfth grade.

"I began my career by teaching art to first through sixth graders in January 1976 at Lawrence Elementary School, filling in for a teacher who was on maternity leave," Lefkovitz recalls. "I was there for one semester, then I taught at Crestview Elementary, also in Lawrence Township, for the next three and one-half years. Upon the arrival of my children, I took a ten-year leave. I returned to the profession in the fall of 1990, when I took a position as a middle school art teacher in Pike Township. The first year, I taught at both Guion Creek Middle School and Lincoln Middle School. For the next three years, I taught exclusively at Lincoln Middle School. During those times, I taught art to sixth through eighth graders. This fall, I will begin my fifth year at Forest Glen Elementary.

"I have always loved the creative process of using the medium of art to express myself," Lefkovitz says. "Paint, crayons, markers, colored pencils, pen and ink, paper, scissors, glue, and pencil have been my companions for all these years. When I was young, I remember being so excited at Christmas because I just knew Santa would bring new art supplies!

"Color is one of my favorite elements of design. From an early age, I was very aware of color and all the many variations of each hue. When I was ready to attend college, I knew I wanted to go to art school. I just wasn't sure what area of art. I had considered commercial art and began as a design major. After two quarters of college, I decided to switch my major to art education. That combined my love of fine arts with my love for children. It has been a perfect combination for me. I still enjoy graphic design, as I have been the yearbook editor for eight years. Teaching others art has been extremely rewarding, and I feel very fortunate in my chosen profession.

"I teach six forty-five-minute classes a day for a total of thirty classes a week. In the morning, I have bus duty. I am in charge of getting all 750 students to their classrooms. At the end of the day, I make sure they get on the correct buses. In between, I live in my classroom. Each day, I teach grades five, four, three, two, and one, in that order.

"Since I teach in an international school, our curriculum is driven by social studies. Each grade level studies a different continent. I teach art with a multicultural focus. My first graders learn about Latin America, second graders travel to Africa and Australia, third graders to Asia, fourth graders go to Europe, and fifth graders study North America. Since the world is full of many cultures and art forms, I literally have the world at my fingertips. In my class, we are all individuals from many cultures, and we value diversity. I also make use of my extensive collection of international dolls to teach art forms and cultures.

"The world is a very colorful place, and we make the most of it. Throughout the year, each child will draw, paint, create a clay piece, cut paper, and use crayon, marker, chalk, and colored pencils. Older children will use ink as well. The topics vary by age and grade, but they all share the same mediums. Each session, I spend about five minutes giving instructions to each class and allow a five-minute cleanup. In between, we create and enjoy! The days are very busy and full. My class is only quiet during instruction and dismissal. Otherwise, we are all learning and sharing. I never sit down and am never bored. After school, I attend meetings. In total, I spend about forty-plus hours a week at school.

"I love the relationships I have with my students and their families. As an art teacher, I have the same students for all five years of elementary school, so I get to really know them well. I am allowed to see them mature and grow up.

"I love art, and I feel that my students learn to share my enthusiasm. Many of them say art is their favorite subject. They have a sense of freedom and expression in my classroom. I emphasize that there is no one way to do anything. The creative process is very important because it involves genuine thinking skills.

"I would highly recommend the field of art education. However, it's important to know that there are considerably fewer art teachers in a school system than there are regular classroom teachers. In fact, some schools don't even have an art teacher. Thus the principle of supply and demand comes into play. So I would suggest that perhaps you might want to have a second area of study as a backup. Most important, I would recommend that you follow your dreams, and if you choose what you love to do, you will be happy."

Professional Associations

Information on teachers' unions and education-related issues may be obtained from:

American Federation of Teachers
555 New Jersey Avenue NW
Washington, DC 20001
www.aft.org

National Education Association
1201 Sixteenth Street NW
Washington, DC 20036
www.nea.org

A list of institutions with teacher education programs accredited by the National Council for Accreditation of Teacher Education is available on the association's website.

National Council for Accreditation of Teacher Education
2010 Massachusetts Avenue NW, Suite 500
Washington, DC 20036
www.ncate.org

For information on teacher certification requirements, contact:

National Board for Professional Teaching Standards
1525 Wilson Boulevard, Suite 500
Arlington, VA 22209
www.nbpts.org

A list of institutions offering training programs in special education may be obtained from:

Council for Exceptional Children
1110 North Glebe Road, Suite 300
Arlington, VA 22201
www.cec.sped.org

For more information on education opportunities, contact:

American Association for Adult and Continuing Education
4380 Forbes Boulevard
Lanham, MD 20706
www.aaace.org

American Association for Higher Education
One Dupont Circle NW, Suite 360
Washington, DC 20036
www.aahe.org

American Association of Christian Schools
2000 Vance Avenue
Chattanooga, TN 37404
www.aacs.org

American Association of Colleges for Teacher Education
1307 New York Avenue NW, Suite 300
Washington, DC 20005
www.aacte.org

American Association of State Colleges and Universities
1307 New York Avenue NW
Washington, DC 20005
www.aascu.org

Association for Childhood Education International
17904 Georgia Avenue, Suite 215
Olney, MD 20832
www.acei.org

Council for American Private Education
13017 Wisteria Drive, #457
Germantown, MD 20874
www.capenet.org

National Association for the Education of Young Children
1509 Sixteenth Street NW
Washington, DC 20036
www.naeyc.org

National Association of Independent Schools
1620 L Street NW, Suite 1100
Washington, DC 20036
www.nais.org

CHAPTER EIGHT

Other Colorful Careers

There is no 'must' in art, because art is free.
—Wassily Kandinsky

The career possibilities for color connoisseurs are limited only by your imagination. The following descriptions of several eclectic career paths for artists should get you started as you explore the unusual and unexpected opportunities available.

CAD Specialist

> **HELP WANTED—CAD OPERATOR**
>
> Manufacturing company seeking experienced CAD operator with HP-ME10 or AUTOCAD R14. Mechanical drafting experience a plus. Send or FAX resume.

Computer-aided design specialists are designers and drafters who use computers rather than pen and paper to produce their work. Working independently, they may specialize in a variety of tasks.

Working Conditions

CAD specialists spend most of their time in offices working in front of computers. This kind of work over the long term may result in eyestrain and/or fatigue. Usually a forty-hour week is required, but overtime can be necessary to meet deadlines.

Training and Qualifications

CAD specialists must have expertise in computer drafting and design. Though this may be taught on the job, most employers require at least a two-year associate's degree in drafting and computer technology.

CAD specialists must be able to work well with others (especially engineers, designers, and architects), be able to meet deadlines, and have excellent communication skills—both verbal and written.

Salaries

Salary levels for CAD specialists vary according to experience and the areas of specialization. Usually, companies offer benefits, such as health insurance, pension plans, and paid holidays and vacations. The median annual salary for CAD specialists is $41,000; the top 10 percent earn $56,260, the lowest 10 percent, $24,570.

Career Outlook

Opportunities for CAD specialists should be best for individuals with at least two years of postsecondary training in a drafting program that provides strong technical skills as well as considerable experience with CAD systems.

The use of CAD technology has increased the complexity of drafting applications while enhancing the productivity of drafters. It also has enhanced the nature of drafting by creating more possibilities for design and drafting.

As technology continues to advance, employers will look for drafters with a strong background in fundamental drafting principles, a higher level of technical sophistication, and an ability to apply their knowledge to a broader range of responsibilities.

Makeup Artist

Theatrical makeup is a means to help convey the personality of the characters in a production to the audience. These artists must use makeup so that audiences are able to clearly view both the expressions and the faces of actors who are on stage.

On the Job

Makeup artists may have different responsibilities, depending on the particular situation. In some productions, characters must be made to look older or younger, and makeup artists must know how to achieve this with cosmetics. Theatrical makeup is generally heavier and more pronounced than everyday makeup. The application will depend on the size and lighting of the theater.

In order to decide on the appropriate makeup, it is important for a theatrical makeup artist to have a complete knowledge of the lighting, staging, and costume design the production will be implementing. Makeup artists must understand the "look" the director is striving for the characters to have.

Makeup artists also work with costume designers and production hair stylists to coordinate colors of makeup with the characters' costumes, hair color, and style.

These artists are responsible for applying the makeup to actors, usually immediately before each performance. Additionally, they are responsible for making changes, touching up, and so on for actors during each performance.

Sometimes theatrical makeup artists function as production hair stylists and keep necessary makeup and supplies stocked for performances.

Job Settings

Employment possibilities include Broadway plays, off-Broadway and off-off-Broadway plays, dinner theater productions, regional theater productions, road shows, cabaret productions, and ballet productions.

Training and Qualifications

Requirements for attaining a position as a makeup artist vary, from a college degree with a major in theater arts to internships, apprenticeships, or on-the-job training. Workshops and seminars are also valuable. In some situations, makeup artists might attend licensed schools of cosmetology and hairstyling to acquire basic skills in this field.

Salaries

Earnings for theatrical makeup artists can vary greatly. Figures depend largely upon experience, abilities, responsibilities, professional reputation, type of production, and amount of work performed each year. Artists may be compensated weekly or by the performance. Junior freelancers working as makeup artists in television and film might get $400 to $600 per day; more experienced freelancers can command $1,200 to $2,000 per day. The International Alliance of Theatrical Stage Employees (IATSE) local union sets the minimum earnings for theatrical makeup artists working on Broadway productions.

Getting Started

Here are some ideas for getting your career as a makeup artist off the ground. All of these experiences could provide valuable experience and contacts.

- Volunteer to handle the makeup for school or college productions.
- Volunteer to help at a local community theater.
- Look for part-time and summer jobs with ballet or opera companies.

- Study makeup by going to a variety of theatrical productions, operas, and ballets.
- Look for apprenticeships and internships with theaters and opera and ballet companies.

Meet Laura Nicholas, Makeup Artist

Laura Nicholas is a makeup artist, licensed esthetician, instructor, and sole proprietor of David Nicholas International, Inc. (DNI, Inc.) After high school, she attended the Elizabeth Grady School of Esthetics, plus various seminars and workshops related to the makeup industry.

"I have always been very fascinated with the art of illusion and with esthetic beauty and fashion," Nicholas says, "and my job is great! My skills are varied to a point where I never get bored. A typical day could involve a photo shoot with a model, then off to do a test at the television station (WBZ-TV). Then I race to the Shriner's Burns Institute Hospital, where I have an existing reconstructive and corrective makeup clinic. There, I'll work with a few patients to teach them how to conceal their burns, scars, whatever. Following that, I will typically do a house call and apply makeup to clients who might be off to the theater, dinner, and so on. I end the day at my Advanced Makeup Training Facility, where I conduct training classes in either basic, advanced, or reconstructive corrective makeup techniques.

"My business can be seasonal; therefore, I do experience some downtime, which I use to promote my business and plan for the busy season. That always includes weddings, teaching, daily clientele, television appearances, speaking at seminars and workshops, and so on. The only dangerous aspect of my career is that I have no time to be sick, so it's important that I stay healthy. I am self-employed and need to plan accordingly for retirement.

"DNI, Inc., is located at the historic Schrafft Center in Charlestown, Massachusetts, near the Bunker Hill Monument.

The atmosphere is very pleasant. The Schrafft Center is an old candy factory that was renovated into a high-profile office complex with all the necessary amenities. I create the atmosphere I work in. I believe that the right positive attitude can make or break your day, your business, or your personal life. I have built DNI into a training facility that is a comfortable, fashionable atmosphere with all the state-of-the-art equipment my clients and students need to learn the art of makeup application and much more.

"The aspect of my career that I love most is the joy of making someone feel great about themselves, whether they are a top model, celebrity, bride, television personality, patient, or student. I also enjoy the daily interaction with people and the diversity of my work. Another aspect of my job that has been rewarding is being duly compensated for the hard work and persistence I have put forth over the past twenty years in building my business.

"The aspect of my work I like the least is retrieving my calls from my answering service. I feel it is important to personally reply to my customers. Depending on the season, and if I have just completed a television appearance or seminar or workshop, I can receive anywhere from thirty to hundreds of calls daily. This can be very labor-intensive due to the fact that I am not always successful in reaching my customers the first time around and, therefore, the telephone-tag syndrome kicks in.

"The advice I would give others would be to stay up to date with industry trends through continued education. And persistence! You cannot stop—keep going no matter how discouraged you may feel. The makeup field is one of madness and beauty."

Art Therapist

Art therapists diagnose and treat patients using a variety of art therapy techniques. The profession is one where psychological and creative arts skills combine to diagnose and treat emotional problems or to encourage self-awareness and personal growth.

Job Settings

Art therapists might work in hospitals, schools, private practices, guidance centers, or nursing homes. Often, art therapists operate as members of therapeutic teams that include psychologists, nurses, occupational therapists, social workers, and psychiatrists. Sessions might involve one or many patients.

Training and Qualifications

These professionals need to be trained in both psychotherapy and art. A variety of techniques and approaches may be applied to art therapy. The underlying principle is that there are emotional benefits that evolve from using art as a medium to express and communicate a host of feelings.

The curriculum for art therapy includes studying the social sciences, behavioral sciences, and the fine arts. Specialized art therapy training also includes studying the history, theory, and practice of art therapy. Any paid or volunteer work involving children, older adults, or emotionally disturbed individuals would be beneficial to those seeking to enter this profession.

Salaries

Median annual income for art therapists ranges from $28,000 to $38,000. Naturally, those who are hired for larger institutions and those with greater expertise and experience are more likely to receive higher annual wages. Earnings for therapists in private practice vary based upon the number of clients they see.

Art therapy is a relatively new and growing field. There are increasing numbers of positions available. Training for art therapy is very specialized and is not offered at many colleges. A core curriculum recognized by the American Art Therapy Association and a master's degree are necessary to work at the professional level.

Trade, Industrial, and Vocational Schools

The following is a list of schools that offer art training. For the most part, they are career oriented and geared to aspiring graphic, commercial, and fine artists.

ALASKA

King Career Center
2650 East Northern Lights Boulevard
Anchorage, AK 99508
www.asdk12.org/schools/kcc/pages

ARIZONA

ITT Technical Institute
5005 South Wendler Drive
Tempe, AZ 85282
www.itt-tech.edu

ITT Technical Institute
1455 West River Road
Tucson, AZ 85704
www.itt-tech.edu

ARKANSAS
Arkansas Arts Center
PO Box 2137
Little Rock, AR 72203
www.arkarts.com

CALIFORNIA
Hollywood Art Center School
2025 North Highland Avenue
Los Angeles, CA 90028

Richmond Art Center
2540 Barrett Avenue
Richmond, CA 94804
www.therichmondartcenter.org

San Francisco Art Institute
800 Chestnut Street
San Francisco, CA 94133
www.sfai.edu

COLORADO
Art Institute of Colorado
1200 Lincoln Street
Denver, CO 80203
www.aic.artinstitutes.edu

Pickens Tech
500 Airport Boulevard
Aurora, CO 80011
www.pickenstech.org

ITT Technical Institute
500 East Eighty-fourth Avenue
Thornton, CO 80229
www.itt-tech.edu

CONNECTICUT
Art Guild
Church Street
Farmington, CT 06032

Paier College of Art
20 Gorham Avenue
Hamden, CT 06514
www.paierart.com

DISTRICT OF COLUMBIA
Corcoran College of Art and Design
500 Seventeenth Street NW
Washington, DC 20006
www.corcoran.edu

FLORIDA
Dixie Hollins Adult Education Center
4940 Sixty-second Street North
St. Petersburg, FL 33709
www.dhaec.pinellas.k12.fl.us

Dunedin Fine Arts and Cultural Center
1143 Michigan Boulevard
Dunedin, FL 34698
www.dfac.org

International Academy of Design and Technology—Tampa
5225 Memorial Highway
Tampa, FL 33634
www.academy.edu

Lindsey Hopkins Education Center
750 Northwest Twentieth Street
Miami, FL 33127
http://lindsey.dadeschools.net

North Miami Adult Education Center
800 Northeast 137th Street
Miami, FL 33161
www.dadeschools.net/schools/nomiami_adult.htm

Remington College—Tampa Campus
2410 East Busch Boulevard
Tampa, FL 33612
www.remingtoncollege.edu

Ringling School of Art and Design
2700 North Tamiami Trail
Sarasota, FL 34234
www.rsad.edu

South Technical Charter High School
1300 Southwest Thirtieth Avenue
Boynton Beach, FL 33426
www.palmbeach.k12.fl.us/SouthTech

Tampa Bay Area Vocational-Technical Center
6410 Orient Road
Tampa, FL 33610

Westside Tech
955 East Story Road
Winter Garden, FL 34787
www.westside.ocps.net

GEORGIA

Atlanta College of Art
Woodruff Art Center
1280 Peachtree Street NE
Atlanta, GA 30309
www.aca.edu

Gertrude Herbert Institute of Art
506 Telfair Street
Augusta, GA 30901
www.ghIa.org

HAWAII

Honolulu Academy of Arts
900 South Beretania Street
Honolulu, HI 96814
www.honoluluacademy.org

ILLINOIS

American Academy of Art
332 South Michigan Avenue
Chicago, IL 60604
www.aaart.edu

Contemporary Art Workshop
542 West Grant Place
Chicago, IL 60614
www.contemporaryartworkshop.org

Peoria Art Guild
203 Harrison Street
Peoria, IL 61602
www.peoriaartguild.org

School of the Art Institute of Chicago
37 South Wabash
Chicago, IL 60603
www.artic.edu

INDIANA
J. Everett Light Career Center
1901 East Eighty-sixth Street
Indianapolis, IN 46240
www.jelcc.com

Tucker Career and Technology Center
107 South Pennsylvania Avenue
Marion, IN 46952
www.tavtc.net

IOWA
Des Moines Art Center
4700 Grand Avenue
Des Moines, IA 50312
www.desmoinesartcenter.org

KANSAS
Kansas City, Kansas Area Technical School
2220 North Fifty-ninth Street
Kansas City, KS 66104
www.kckats.com

LOUISIANA
Sowela Technical Community College
3820 Legion Street
Lake Charles, LA 70616
www.sowela.net

MARYLAND
Carver Vocational-Technical High School
2201 Pressman Street
Baltimore, MD 21216

Mergenthaler Vocational-Technical High School
3500 Hillen Road
Baltimore, MD 21218
http://mergenthaler.baltimorecityschools.org

Schuler School of Fine Arts
7 East Lafayette Avenue
Baltimore, MD 21202
www.auronet.com/schuler

MASSACHUSETTS
Art Institute of Boston
700 Beacon Street
Boston, MA 02215
www.aiboston.edu

Blue Hills Regional Technical School
800 Randolph Street
Canton, MA 02021
www.bluehills.org

Butera School of Art
111 Beacon Street
Boston, MA 02116
www.buteraschool.com

New England School of Art and Design
Suffolk University
75 Arlington Street
Boston, MA 02116
www.suffolk.edu/nesad

New Art Center in Newton
61 Washington Park
Newtonville, MA 02160
www.newartcenter.org

School of the Museum of Fine Arts
230 The Fenway
Boston, MA 02115
www.smfa.edu

Whittier Regional Vocational Technical High School
115 Amesbury Line Road
Haverhill, MA 01830
www.whittier.mec.edu

MICHIGAN
College for Creative Studies
201 East Kirby
Detroit, MI 48202
www.ccscad.edu

MISSOURI

Kansas City Art Institute
4415 Warwick Boulevard
Kansas City, MO 64111
www.kcai.edu

NEW HAMPSHIRE

New Hampshire Institute of Art
148 Concord Street
Manchester, NH 03104
www.nhia.edu

NEW JERSEY

Arts High School
550 Martin Luther King Boulevard
Newark, NJ 07102
www.nps.k12.nj.us/arts/default.htm

Atlantic County Vocational-Technical School
5080 Atlantic Avenue
Mays Landing, NJ 08330
www.acitech.org

Linden Vo-Tech High School
128 West Saint George Avenue
Linden, NJ 07036
www.linden.k12.nj.us

Middlesex County Vo-Tech
112 Rues Lane
East Brunswick, NY 08816
www.mc-votech.org/schools/eb.asp

Passaic County Vocational School
45 Reinhardt Road
Wayne, NJ 07470
www.pcti.tec.nj.us

NEW YORK
Art Students League of New York
215 West Fifty-seventh Street
New York, NY 10019
www.theartstudentsleague.org

National Academy Museum and School of Fine Arts
5 East Eighty-ninth Street
New York, NY 10128
www.nationalacademy.org

New York Academy of Art
111 Franklin Street
New York, NY 10013
www.nyaa.edu

New York Studio School of Drawing, Painting, and Sculpture
8 West Eighth Street
New York, NY 10011
www.nyss.org

NORTH CAROLINA
Mint Museum of Art
2730 Randolph Road
Charlotte, NC 28207
www.mintmuseum.org

Sawtooth Center for Visual Design
226 North Marshall Street, Suite D
Winston-Salem, NC 27101
www.sawtooth.org

OHIO
Antonelli College
124 East Seventh Street
Cincinnati, OH 45202
www.antonellicollege.edu

Art Academy of Cincinnati
1125 Saint Gregory Street
Cincinnati, OH 45202
www.artacademy.edu

College of Art Advertising
4343 Bridgetown Road
Cincinnati, OH 45211
http://collegeofartadvertising.com

Cincinnati Academy of Design
2181 Victory Parkway, #200
Cincinnati, OH 45206

Fine Arts Association
38660 Mentor Avenue
Willoughby, OH 44094
www.fineartsassociation.org

PENNSYLVANIA
Art Institute of Philadelphia
1622 Chestnut Street
Philadelphia, PA 19103
www.aiph.artinstitutes.edu

Art Institute of Pittsburgh
420 Boulevard of the Allies
Pittsburgh, PA 15219
www.aip.aii.edu

Hussian School of Art
1118 Market Street
Philadelphia, PA 19107
www.hussianart.edu

Greater Altoona Career and Technology Center
1500 Fourth Avenue
Altoona, PA 16602
www.gactc.com

Lancaster County Career and Technology Center—
   Brownstown Campus
Visual Communications Center
PO Box 519
Brownstown, PA 17508
www.lcctc.org

Lancaster County Career and Technology Center
   —Mount Joy Campus
432 Old Market Street
Mount Joy, PA 17552
www.lcctc.org

Pennsylvania Academy of Fine Arts
1301 Cherry Street
Philadelphia, PA 19107
www.pafa.org/educate.jsp

Pittsburgh Technical Institute
1111 McKee Road
Oakdale, PA 15071
www.pittsburghtechnical.com

RHODE ISLAND
Rhode Island School of Design
Two College Street
Providence, RI 02903
www.risde.edu

SOUTH CAROLINA
Museum School of Art
420 College Street
Greenville, SC 29601
www.greenvillemuseum.org/school.html

TENNESSEE
Memphis College of Art
1930 Poplar Avenue
Memphis, TN 38104
www.mca.edu

Nossi College of Art
907 Rivergate Parkway
Goodlettsville, TN 37072
www.nossi.com

TEXAS
Texas State Technical College Waco
3801 Campus Drive
Waco, TX 76705
www.waco.tstc.edu

UTAH
Salt Lake Art Center
20 South West Temple
Salt Lake City, UT 84101
www.slartcenter.org

VERMONT
North Country Career Center
209 Veterans Avenue
Newport, VT 05855
www.ncuhs.org/careercenter.html

WASHINGTON
Bellevue Arts Museum
510 Bellevue Way NE
Bellevue, WA 98004
www.bellevueart.org

Pratt Fine Arts Center
1902 South Main Street
Seattle, WA 98144
www.pratt.org

New School of Visual Concepts
500 Aurora Avenue North
Seattle, WA 98109
www.svcseattle.com

WISCONSIN
Racine Art Museum
441 Main Street
Racine, WI 53401
www.ramart.org

About the Author

Jan Goldberg's love for the printed page began well before her second birthday. Regular visits to the book bindery where her grandfather worked produced a magic combination of sights and smells that she carries with her to this day.

Childhood was filled with composing poems and stories, reading books, and playing library. Elementary and high school included an assortment of contributions to school newspapers. While a full-time college student, Goldberg wrote extensively as part of her job responsibilities in the College of Business Administration at Roosevelt University in Chicago. After receiving a degree in elementary education, she was able to extend her love of reading and writing to her students.

Goldberg has written extensively in the occupations area for *Career World Magazine,* as well as for the many career publications produced by CASS Communications. She has also contributed to a number of projects for educational publishers, including Scott Foresman, Addison-Wesley, and Camp Fire Boys and Girls.

As a feature writer, Goldberg's work has appeared in *Parenting, Today's Chicago Woman, Chicago Parent, Correspondent, Successful Student, Complete Woman, North Shore Magazine,* and the Pioneer Press newspapers. In all, she has published more than 250 pieces as a freelance writer.

In addition to *Careers for Color Connoisseurs,* she is the author of *Careers for Class Clowns, Great Jobs for Music Majors, Great Jo*[*]* for Computer Science Majors, Great Jobs for Theater Majors, Car*[*]* for Courageous People, Careers in Journalism,* and *Great Job*[*]* Accounting Majors,* all published by McGraw-Hill.